PRACTICING TRUTH IN THE FAMILY OF GOD

A Study of Hebrews, Chapters 11-13

by Eva Gibson

A Bible Study

Women's Aglow Fellowship International
P.O. Box 1548
Lynnwood, WA 98046-1548
USA

Cover design by Paz Design Group

Women's Aglow Fellowship International, is an interdenominational organization of Christian women. Our mission is to lead women to Jesus Christ and provide opportunity for Christian women to grow in their faith and minister to others.

Our publications are used to help women find a personal relationship with Jesus Christ, to enhance growth in their Christian experience, and to help them recognize their roles and relationship according to Scripture.

For more information about our organization, please write to Women's Aglow Fellowship International, P.O. Box 1548, Lynnwood, WA 98046-1548, USA, or call (206) 775-7282.

Unless otherwise noted all scripture quotations are from the New King James Version (NKJV). Copyright ©1979, 1980, 1982, Thomas Nelson, Inc. Other versions are abbreviated as follows: New American Standard Bible (NASB), New International Version (NIV), The Amplified Bible (TAB), and The Living Bible (TLB).

© Copyright 1995, Eva Gibson. Published by Women's Aglow Fellowship International, Lynnwood, Washington, USA. All rights reserved. Except for brief quotations for review purposes, no part of this book may be reproduced in any form or by any electronic or mechanical means without prior permission from the publisher. Printed in the United States of America.

ISBN 1-56616-012-X

1 2 3 4 Printing/Year 97 96 95

AGLOW BIBLE STUDIES

Basic Series

God's Daughter
Practical Aspects of a Christian Woman's Life

The Holy Spirit and His Gifts
A Study of the Spiritual Gifts

Coming Alive in the Spirit
The Spirit-Led Life

Discovering the Heart of God Series

Called to Spiritual Maturity
A Study of Hebrews, Chapters 1-4

Getting to Know the Heart of God
A Study of Hebrews, Chapters 5-10

Practicing Truth in the Family of God
A Study of Hebrews, Chapters 11-13

Write for a free catalog

For important NEW information on how to order a Leader's Guide for all three Bible studies of Hebrews by Eva Gibson, please see next page.

How to Order a *Leader's Guide*

We have just made the ordering process for a Bible study Leader's Guide as easy as dialing the phone! The Aglow order number, 1-800-755-2456, puts you right through to us.

Now you will be able to order one or more Leader's Guides at the same time you order from our warehouse and you will be billed $1. for each Leader's Guide on your Aglow invoice. We encourage you to order Leader's Guides at the same time you order other Aglow materials to save additional charges.

Dedicated to

my husband, Bud

A special thank you to Debbie Scufca and Wendall Hollis
of BEE (Bible Education by Extension)
in Vienna, Austria.

God used her encouragement to challenge
me to write beyond myself.
God used his encouragement and theological expertise
to keep me persevering through the book of Hebrews.

Contents

Introduction		9
Chapter 1	Faith Is . . . Hebrews 10:32–11:7	13
Chapter 2	An Adventure in Faith Hebrews 11:8-19	27
Chapter 3	Faith for the Family Hebrews 11:20-29	43
Chapter 4	A Faith That Endures Hebrews 11:30-40	59
Chapter 5	Running the Race Hebrews 12:1-13	77
Chapter 6	Keep on Running Hebrews 12:14-28	91
Chapter 7	Let Love Continue Hebrews 13:1-10	107
Chapter 8	Grace Be with You All Hebrews 13:11-25	123

Introduction

The book of Hebrews captured my heart almost from the first time I read the words, "God . . . has in these last days spoken to us by His Son." I sat very still. Jesus Christ, the Son of God who died for me wanted to speak to me. A heavenly wonder filled me.

I know now that Hebrews is a difficult book. But the truths that walk across its pages are rich and beautiful.

Chapters 1–4: Jesus Christ, greater than the prophets, the angels, Moses. These chapters are like a symphony. Their glory pulls me close to God.

Chapters 5–10: Jesus Christ, greater than the Jewish sacrificial system, greater than the high priest. Jesus Christ, the sacrificial Lamb . . .

Darkness. Tears. The world waits. . . .

Cymbals crash. Silence.

Hebrews 11

And out of the silence comes a song. A single faith note rises into the air. Abel brings an offering.

Another note. Enoch walks with God.

More faith notes. A hammer pounds. A boat rises in the hills. Abraham, Sarah, Moses.

More faith notes. . . . Real people walk across the desert. People of hope. People of faith.

"Now faith is the substance of things hoped for, the evidence of things not seen" (Heb. 11:1).

Soar, Run, Walk

Once the writer of Hebrews established Christ's superiority in the first ten chapters, he shifted his emphasis to people. Someone as excellent as Jesus Christ deserves wholehearted faith.

It took faith for the men and women of old to live their lives with God. But some of them did. Because they did, they leave footprints for us to follow. Footprints that show us how to live our lives as twentieth century women.

"Therefore, strengthen your feeble arms and weak knees. 'Make level paths for your feet,' so that the lame may not be disabled, but rather healed (Heb. 12:12-13 NIV).

Hebrews 11—13 gives feet to faith and wings to hope. We can soar. We can run.

We can walk together, one step at a time.

How to Use This Book:

This study is designed to help you grow in your understanding of the heart of God. Each study is in four parts:

1. *God Speaks* is an inductive study.

2. *I Listen* has suggestions adapted to journaling to help you apply the truth you're learning to specific areas in your life.

3. *We Talk Together* has encouragment and suggestions for prayer and praise.

4. *Walking Along Together* shows how God made each week's scripture passage real to the author.

The study is designed to be done a little each day, five days a week. You will profit most if you take the time to daily ask the Holy Spirit to be your teacher before you begin.

Use each day's study questions to work through the scripture passage. They will prepare you to make daily application in the *I Listen* and help you present your praise and prayers to God in *We Talk Together* with deepened insight. The narrative section is to be read at the end of the week after you have completed all five sections.

You will need this study guide, the New King James Version (NKJV) Bible translation, a notebook, and/or your journal, dictionary, and concordance.

It would be good to have a commentary, Bible dictionary, and several Bible translations.

If you're part of a group, you'll find it most helpful to complete the study questions before you meet. Solidify what you're learning by being ready to share what you've learned and how it applies to your life. Write down any unanswered questions you may have. Your leader or others in the group may be able to help you further.

For Leaders, A Guide

The book of Hebrews is written to women whom God wants to draw into a deeper relationship with Himself. Women who have problems, women who want to reflect the heart of God. Woman who want to grow in their faith and practice God's truth in practical ways in their relationships with others.

These last three chapters will challenge you to put feet to what you believe. You've taken a giant step in Christian maturity by choosing to study them.

If you wish to order a *Leader's Guide* for this study, please turn to page 4.

1

Faith Is . . .

Hebrews 10:32–11:7

❦ DAY 1 ❦

GOD SPEAKS

FAITH FOR THE FAMILY OF GOD

    A man brought before a judge in the early days of Christianity told the judge that nothing anyone could do to him could shake his faith in God. "Do you really think you will go to God and His glory?" the judge asked. "I do not think," the man said. "I know."

1. How would you describe this man's faith?

_____

How does it compare with your own?

_____

Practicing Truth in the Family of God

2. Over the centuries, many have called Hebrews 11, the faith chapter. But what is faith really? Quickly jot down a thought you have about faith by completing this sentence, "Faith is . . . .

   _____

The writer of Hebrews actually introduces the subject of faith in chapter 10. He even describes the original readers as men and women of faith.
   Read **Hebrews 10:32–11:2.**

3. What three things do you discover about these believers in verses 32-34?

   a. _____

   b. _____

   c. _____

4. The believers in these verses have showed themselves to be men and women of faith. Compare the last part of verse 34 with Hebrews 11:1. What evidences of faith do you see in these verses?

   _____

5. Faith looks into the future. According to verses 34-36, what will faithful believers receive?

   a. _____

   b. _____

   How do do these things give us strength to endure?

   _____

   _____

Faith Is . . .

6. The writer likes to use contrasts in his writing. In verse 38 he contrasts the just (righteous) one who _____ to a person who _____ (v. 39).

    But the writer was convinced these believers had chosen the way of faith. Why do you think this is so?

    _____

    _____

Read Hebrews 11:1-2 in as many different translations as possible. For example the Amplified Bible says, "Now faith is the assurance (the confirmation, the title-deed) of the things [we] hope for, being the proof of things [we] do not see and the conviction of their reality — faith perceiving as real fact what is not revealed to the senses. For by [faith], and trust and holy fervor born of faith, the men of old had divine testimony borne to them and obtained a good report."

7. In what way is the writer's definition of faith in Hebrews 11:1 similar or different with what you wrote about faith at the beginning of today's study?

    _____

    _____

8. What effect do you want faith to have on your walk with God?

    _____

I LISTEN

There is nothing more precious than faith in the family of God—it is by faith that we obtain a good testimony. But faith doesn't have opportunity to grow unless we endure hard things. Read the following quotation from Charles Swindoll.

> The word endurance in verse 36 is from the Greek verb *hupomeno*. It means "abiding under, staying with it, not giving up or giving in." Endurance is what gives us a second wind and

Practicing Truth in the Family of God

a will to go on. And that comes through faith. The alternative to faith? To "shrink back." The word is *hupostellō*. It is the opposite of *hupomeno*. It means "to retreat, to find a way out."[1]

Write a letter to God in your journal. Describe a difficulty you're going through right now. Do you sometimes feel like giving up instead of "staying with it"? Shrinking back instead of moving forward?

Tell it like it is.

WE TALK TOGETHER

Read Mark 9:24. Make the words of the father in this account your prayer. Ask God to give you a faith that continues.

❦ DAY 2 ❦

GOD SPEAKS

FAITH AND CREATION

1. How would you define creation?

   _____

   How would you define faith?

   _____

   Why is it easier to define something seen rather than something unseen?

   _____

   _____

---

1. Charles R. Swindoll, *The Practical Life of Faith* (Anaheim, CA: Insight for Living, 1989), p. 4.

Faith Is . . .

Read **Hebrews 11:1-3.**
2. What is the author saying in these verses?

___

What is he saying about it?

___

William Barclay says faith is, "a hope that has turned to certainty."[2] "Now faith is being sure of what we hope for and certain of what we do not see. This is what the ancients were commended for" (Heb. 11:1-2 NIV).

3. What two words in verse 1 speak of deep inner conviction?

___

4. Verses 2-3 take us back into Genesis. What do your friends believe about creation?

___

Why does it take faith to believe in the Genesis account?

___

Why do you think the writer of Hebrews begins his splendid theme of faith by mentioning creation?

___

5. Compare Hebrews 11:3 with the following scriptures. What more do you discover about faith and creation?

Hebrews 1:2 ___

---

2. William Barclay, *The Letter to the Hebrews* (Philadelphia, PA: Westminster Press, 1976), p. 128.

Practicing Truth in the Family of God

Romans 1:20 _____

Psalm 33:6 _____

Psalm 33:9 _____

No one was present at creation, there were no eyewitness reports. Therefore, it is by _____
that we ascertain that God created the universe.

I LISTEN

It is difficult for modern men, women, and children to accept the Genesis account of the origin of the world. What about you? Putting into words in your journal what you believe about creation will strengthen your faith. It will help you become more confident of God and His Word.

WE TALK TOGETHER

What do you envision today that you are confident God will one day make visible? Talk to God about it.

❦ DAY 3 ❦

GOD SPEAKS

ABEL'S FAITH

1. Have you ever known or read about someone who demonstrated faith by the things she did? Choose the incident that was most memorable and be ready to tell about it.

One reason the writer of Hebrews uses illustrations from the lives of real people is that faith takes on substance only when displayed in human flesh. His method was to select notable men and women, then show how faith was worked out in practical ways in their lives. The first illustration is Abel.

Faith Is . . .

Read **Hebrews 11:4**.
2. Write down several observations about Abel's faith from this verse.

_____

_____

Read **Genesis 4:1-11**.
3. Cain is a negative example of faith; Abel, a positive one. Write down as many observations as you can about the brothers and their sacrifices:

Cain	Abel

Which contrast between the two brothers is most significant to you? Why?

_____

_____

Many have wondered why Abel's sacrifice was accepted and Cain's wasn't.

Read **Hebrews 9:11-14** and **Genesis 3:21**.
4. Why do you think Abel's sacrifice was acceptable to God and Cain's wasn't?

_____

From the very beginning man has tried to come to God in his own way, by the works of his own hands. But God's way has always been through the shed blood of a sacrifice. Jesus, God's only Son, is God's ultimate sacrifice.

Practicing Truth in the Family of God

Read **Hebrews 11:4** again.

5. What unusual observation does the writer make about the quality of Abel's faith?

   _____

   What observation would you like God to make about the quality of your faith?

   _____

I LISTEN

What single truth has most impacted you about Abel's faith? Think about his sacrifice and worship, his obedience and righteousness. Explore your thoughts on the pages of your journal.

WE TALK TOGETHER

Ask God to show you His way for you today. Praise Jesus for being The Way, the Truth, and the Life.

🌱 DAY 4 🌱

GOD SPEAKS

ENOCH'S FAITH

1. A young woman cried, "Oh, I could be the most perfect Christian if I just didn't have a husband and children." Have you ever felt this way? Explain.

   _____

   Why is it sometimes so difficult to honor God in the way we live when we live with other people?

   _____

Faith Is . . .

Read **Hebrews 11:5-6.**
2. Who is this man who walked so close to God that he walked into heaven without dying? What was there about him that so pleased God?

_____

_____

When the writer says, "and was not found because God had translated him," he is repeating the conclusion of the verses in Genesis that give his genealogy.

Read **Genesis 5:21-24.**
3. In these verses Enoch's life is summed up in one sentence. What is it?

_____

What else do you discover about Enoch from these verses?

_____

Enoch demonstrates that it's possible to walk faithfully with God even when we have sons and daughters. What positive effects can children have on a person's walk with God?

_____

What negative effects?

_____

Read **Jude 14-15.**
4. What else do you discover about Enoch?

_____

Practicing Truth in the Family of God

Enoch proclaimed a message that his wicked generation resented. What message did God give him?

_____

God gives us all a message from His Word to give to someone. What message is He laying on your heart for others?

_____

I LISTEN

Anytime we see a word, a form of a word, or a phrase recurring in scripture we need to take note. The phrase, "Enoch walked with God" is repeated twice in Genesis 5. What does this phrase mean? Write down several observations about faith and walking with God from today's study. How would you like them to affect your walk with God? Your walk with your family?

WE TALK TOGETHER

Walking with God means we trust Him and confide in Him as our closest friend. Tell Him all about whatever is closest to your heart today.

❦ DAY 5 ❦

GOD SPEAKS

NOAH'S FAITH

1. Think back to your childhood. What details do you remember about Noah and the ark?

   _____

   What part of the story most impressed you as a child?

   _____

Faith Is . . .

What part of the story impresses you most as an adult (Gen. 6–9)?

_____

Yesterday we learned about Enoch who walked with God. Noah is another man of whom it is written, "Noah walked with God" (Gen. 6:9).

Read Genesis 6:5, 11-13.
2. Describe the society that surrounded Noah and his family.

_____

How is it similar to our society today?

_____

Read Genesis 6:8-9, 22; 7:5, 9, 16.
3. Describe Noah.

_____

Describe his work.

_____

Read Hebrews 11:7.
4. Find a phrase in the verse that matches the following statements about faith.

Faith is listening to God. _____

Faith is working with God. _____

5. Noah's attitude toward his work gives us insight into his relationship with God. What words does the writer use to describe it?

_____

Practicing Truth in the Family of God

What else do you observe about Noah's faith in this verse?

_____

6. Abel, Enoch, and Noah were ordinary men who lived lives of extraordinary faith. Finish the following sentences in your own words:

   By faith Abel _____

   By faith Enoch _____

   By faith Noah _____

Challenge activity: Read **Hebrews 11.** Whenever you come to the word *faith* underline it.

How many *faiths* did you find? _____

List all the names of the Old Testament heroes of faith.

_____

_____

How many are there? _____

I LISTEN
Women who live by faith do things God's way. Women who walk by faith keep going. Women who work by faith undertake big tasks.

What task is God revealing to you that would take a faith like Noah's to complete? What step can you take today that will move you forward in this specific area?

WE TALK TOGETHER
In many ways, growing mature in faith means becoming like a little child (Matt. 18:1-4). Jesus invites you to come now and climb into His lap. You can tell Him your dreams, your hopes. He wants to strengthen you so you can walk with Him, one faith step at a time.

Faith Is . . .

WALKING ALONG TOGETHER

Faith is . . . I like to write those words on a piece of butcher paper with a bright red felt tip pen when I teach teens about faith. I tack it on the wall and watch to see what they write.

Faith is . . . Mandie hesitates, then writes, *"something I can't see."* B.J. selects a black pen. *Faith is* . . . He writes, *"a leap in the dark, only no one's there."* Jeni selects a red, a blue, and a green pen. *Faith is* . . . *"like a rainbow. Now you see it, now you don't."*

Michael protests. "It's impossible to write about something you can't put in words. It's stupid."

I nod. As a writer I've struggled with that concept often enough. I also know the Bible has a lot to say about faith, especially Hebrews 11. *Faith is* . . . Andrea writes *"hope dressed up."*

Anticipation sparks in me. I found *hope* in a Bible dictionary yesterday. I read something like this: "Faith, hope, and love are inseparable. Hope cannot exist apart from faith, and love cannot be exercised without hope. These three are the things that . . . together comprise the Christian way of life."

Faith is . . . Darci writes, *"love in action."*

She smiles at me. "There," she said, "that's it. We can go home now."

Faith, hope . . .

After class I linger in the room. *Faith* . . . *hope* . . . It's something I've always suspected whenever I've read Hebrews 11. Faith is the outward evidence of the hope planted by the Holy Spirit within a believer's heart. That hope radiates upward and outward and moves a person to respond to God's word and reach out to others. *Faith is* . . . I pick up a green pen, *"hope in action."*

It's almost like the rainbows I used to chase when I was a child. Oh, I knew I could never find the rainbow's end. At least I never did. And as for the pot of gold—it was only a pretty tale. But I ran just the same.

Before I go to the worship service, I reach for a yellow pen, draw a golden pot with wings. Alongside I write, *"Faith gives hope wings."*

A Rainbow of Faith

I sit in the worship service. God Himself is the Light of the World; we, His children, are His prisms. The unique shape and color of each

Practicing Truth in the Family of God

prism is a reflection of each person's faith, her ministry, personality, talents, environment, heritage, interests, and spiritual gifts filtered through the presence of the Holy Spirit.

I look around me. Randy looks more interested in sleep than he does in singing praises. And I know that Bob lost his temper yesterday when he pounded the table and shouted at Lucy.

But how does God see us? "And we, who with unveiled faces all reflect the Lord's glory, are being transformed into his likeness with ever-increasing glory, which comes from the Lord, who is the Spirit" (2 Cor. 3:18 NIV).

I turn to Hebrews 11. Is Abel's faith a soft blue with a lavender hue? Is Enoch's faith a royal blue that gets richer and deeper with each step he takes? Noah's, a multi-colored bow arched above a water-washed world?

Just as no two prisms reflect the same colors in quite the same way or in the same place, neither can one person's faith be duplicated by another. God has made each of us into a one-of-a-kind person with a one-of-a-kind-God-designed ministry.

"And what more shall I say? For the time would fail me to tell of Gideon and Barak and Samson and Jephthah, also of David and Samuel and the prophets: who through faith subdued kingdoms, worked righteousness, obtained promises, stopped the mouths of lions, quenched the violence of fire, escaped the edge of the sword, out of weakness were made strong, became valiant in battle, turned to flight the armies of aliens" (Heb. 11:32-34).

Suddenly I know. When we all unite together—the saints of the past, the saints of the present and the future—we'll make a reflection of the greater rainbow in heaven, the one encircling God's throne (Rev. 4:3). We can do it now as we serve others at home, at church, at work, and in the neighborhood. I open my notebook and write:

Faith is . . . a prism of hope.

Faith is . . . God's people reflecting love into a darkened world.

Faith is . . . love in action, fulfilling God's Word.

"Now we see but a poor reflection as in a mirror; then we shall see face to face. . . . And now these three remain: faith, hope and love. But the greatest of these is love" (1 Cor. 13:12-13 NIV).

2

An Adventure in Faith

Hebrews 11:8-19

❧ DAY 1 ❧

GOD SPEAKS

ABRAHAM'S FAITH

1. Describe an adventure you once had. What particular qualities made it an adventure?

   _____

   _____

   _____

   _____

Practicing Truth in the Family of God

Read **Hebrews 11:8-10.**
2. What do you remember most about Abraham?

_____

Read **Genesis 11:29–13:4.**
3. Write down what you think might be symptoms of fear in Abraham and what could be characterized as steps of faith.

_____

_____

Read **Hebrews 11:8-10** again.
4. Write down 6-10 observations. Suggestions: note verbs, names, nouns, pronouns, important words, etc. Ask yourself, How does Abraham see God?

_____

_____

_____

_____

Put a star by the observation you think is most important. Explain why you chose it.

_____

Read **Genesis 12:1-8**.
5. Although Abraham's early walk with God was characterized by fear, he is remembered for his faithfulness. Compare this Genesis passage with Hebrews 11:8-10. What speaks to you about Abraham's faithfulness in this instance?

_____

An Adventure in Faith

His fearfulness?

_____

Summarize what you feel is the most important lesson for you in these verses.

_____

I LISTEN

Explore the following questions in your journal: How might fear keep you from embarking on an adventure with God? Is there an area in your life that you are afraid to entrust to Him? A certain situation in which you long to move from fearfulness to faithfulness? Ask the Holy Spirit to give you insight as you think these things through with Him.

WE TALK TOGETHER

Abraham trusted God even when God didn't make sense. What about you? Do you dare to trust and obey Him even when the pieces don't fit together? Are you ready to ask Him to make your life an adventure with Him?

🎔 DAY 2 🎔

GOD SPEAKS

Sarah's Faith

Read **Hebrews 11:11-12.**
1. Has God ever called you to believe the impossible? How did it make you feel? What did you learn about faith through it?

_____

_____

_____

Practicing Truth in the Family of God

Abram's eyes were fixed on a distant horizon. God had talked to him and he had listened. "Get out of your country," God had said. So Abram departed as the LORD had spoken to him (Gen. 12:4).

2. Gradually God revealed to Abram more about what He wanted to do in and through Abram. What specifically is God promising to do for Abram in the following scriptures?

   Genesis 13:14-16 _____

   Genesis 15:1-5 _____

   Genesis 17:1-7 _____

3. But what about Sarah? What do you remember most about Abraham's wife?

   _____

   Compare what you remember with the following scriptures. What more do you discover about Sarah?

   1 Peter 3:6 _____

   Genesis 18:9-19 _____

   Hebrews 11:11-12 _____

   Put an asterisk beside the two scriptures that appear to contradict each other.

Read **Genesis 21:1-7** and **Hebrews 11:11-12.**
4. What do you think happened inside Sarah's heart that changed her laughter of unbelief (Gen. 18:12) to that of belief (Gen. 21:6)?

   _____

An Adventure in Faith

What hope does this give you?

_____

5. What more do you learn about God's faithfulness in these passages?

_____

How does His faithfulness strengthen your faith?

_____

Read **Romans 10:17**.
6. What more do you learn about faith?

_____

I LISTEN

Years passed before Abraham and Sarah received the son they had been promised. Sometimes they saw clearly. Other times they doubted.

What has God given you faith to believe from His Word? What vision has He given you to pursue? Quickly list (no longer than three minutes allowed here) some of the doubts that cause your faith in God and His Word to crumble.

Across your list write in big bold letters, GOD IS FAITHFUL. Read Hebrews 11:12, then finish this sentence in your own words, "Therefore . . ."

WE TALK TOGETHER

Read Genesis 17:15-21. Did Abraham and Sarah see all the descendants God had promised? The kings God would raise up in their family? Ask God to give you the courage to trust Him even though years may pass before His promises to you are fulfilled.

Practicing Truth in the Family of God

❦ DAY 3 ❦

GOD SPEAKS

THE EYES OF FAITH

Read **Hebrews 11:13-16.**
1. Describe a place or a time you would like to return to some day. What is it that makes you want to go back?

_____

_____

_____

Most commentators think that "these all" refer to Abraham, Sarah, Isaac, and Jacob. These all received the promise concerning the land of Canaan, yet they remained tent dwellers; these all were given the promise of innumerable offspring, yet while they lived they only saw sons and grandsons.

2. What does this tell you about the quality of their faith?

_____

3. The details the writer of Hebrews gives about Abraham reveal him as a man of vision. Look back at Hebrews 11:9-10. According to these verses, what was the point of Abraham's focus?

_____

What more do you discover about Abraham's vision in the following verses?

Hebrews 11:12 _____

Hebrews 11:13 _____

An Adventure in Faith

Hebrews 11:14 _____

Hebrews 11:15 _____

Read **Hebrews 12:22-23.**
4. What additional details does the writer of Hebrews give about the heavenly city Abraham and Sarah saw from a distance?

_____

5. Compare the focus of Abraham's life to what Paul expresses in Colossians 3:1-3.

If then you have been raised with Christ [to a new life, thus sharing His resurrection from the dead], aim at and seek the [rich, eternal treasures] that are above, where Christ is, seated at the the right hand of God. And set your minds and keep them set on what is above—the higher things—not on the things that are on the earth. For [as far as this world is concerned] you have died, and your [new, real] life is hid with Christ in God. (Col. 3:1-3 TAB).

Which did Abraham see most clearly—the things of earth or the things of heaven? Explain your answer.

_____

Compare your own life focus to the same verses. What has the highest demand on your priorities? The earthly or the heavenly?

_____

Abraham and Sarah's faith moved them to do two things: (1) They actively pursued what they saw by faith. (2) They refused to dwell on what they had in the past.

Rather than fretting about what they had left behind, they totally abandoned themselves to follow God's Word. They didn't even consider going back to their original home in Ur.

Practicing Truth in the Family of God

6. How did they do it? Hebrews 11:16 gives us a clue in the word: *desire*. What does it mean to desire something or someone with all your heart? Quickly jot down the synonyms/words/ phrases that come to your mind.

   _____

   Look up *desire* in a dictionary. What additional insights do you find?

   _____

Read **Psalm 37:4-7**.
7. How do these verses reflect Abraham and Sarah's lives?

   _____

   Their desires?

   _____

   How would you like to see these verses reflected in your own life?

   _____

I LISTEN

How is your vision? Review Colossians 3:1-3, then read Philippians 3:17-21. Explore some practical—and creative—suggestions you could give to someone who wanted to make the eternal rather than the earthly her focus.

Try at least one of them out yourself! You'll be glad you did!

WE TALK TOGETHER

What are your innermost desires? The man who wrote Psalm 42 knew what it was like to desire God—to long after, reach out for, and yearn for Him with his whole heart. Read verses 1 and 2. Ask God to help you make the psalmist's words the desire of your heart. Paraphrasing these verses into your own words will make them your own.

An Adventure in Faith

❦ DAY 4 ❦

GOD SPEAKS

THE TEST OF FAITH

Read **Hebrews 11:17-19.**
1. How do you think you would feel if God asked you to give up the most important person in your life: a husband, child, parent, a friend, or a favorite uncle, etc.?

_____

The Christian life is a series of tests, some moderate, some severe. It was like that for Abraham. Leaving his homeland, waiting for a child, rescuing Lot. But his ultimate test came when he faced the loss of his son. Genesis 22 tells the story.

Read **Genesis 22:1-5.**
The Hebrew verb stem used in the word *test* (v. 1) conveys the most intense meaning of pain. Try to imagine how Abraham felt when he heard the next words spoken by the God he loved (v. 2), the God he had sought to obey all his life.

2. Write a description of what you think his feelings might have been.

_____

3. In spite of his emotions and the questions that must have hammered inside him, his response was immediate obedience. (vv. 3-5.) What does this tell you about his trust in God?

_____

How does his use of the pronoun "we" (v. 5) further express his confidence in God?

_____

Practicing Truth in the Family of God

Read **Genesis 22:6-18.**

4. Abraham expressed his faith in God's ability to provide when he told Isaac, _____ (v. 8). God honored his faith by providing a _____ (v. 13). He further confirmed His blessing to Abraham by promising _____ and _____.

Read **Hebrews 11:17-19** again.

5. What additional insights does the writer of Hebrews bring to the Genesis account of Abraham and Isaac on Mount Moriah?

   _____

   What is he saying about it?

   _____

6. Ultimate tests are an important part of growing in spiritual maturity. What has God taught you through the loss of someone or something that was near and dear to you? It could even be the loss of a dream or something you considered valuable.

   _____

I LISTEN

What was the secret of Abraham's confidence in God? The writer of Hebrews gives a clue in his use of the word *accounting* (Heb. 11:19). Abraham brought God into his reasoning. He knew what it meant to think things through with God—even the things that didn't make sense.

What a person understands about God affects the quality of his faith. Look back over the scriptures you studied today. See God through Abraham's eyes. Which specific truth about Him touches you most deeply?

WE TALK TOGETHER

Ask God to give you the insights you need from His Word that will help you develop a triumphant faith.

An Adventure in Faith

❧ DAY 5 ❧

GOD SPEAKS

A CALL FOR PERSEVERANCE IN FAITH

Read **Hebrews 11:8-19.**

1. Look up the word *adventure* in a dictionary. What words and phrases do you think particularly apply to Abraham?

   _____

   How would you like them to apply to your life?

   _____

2. Choose a verse or a key principle from each day's scripture passage that particularly impressed you. Use your discovery to help you create a new title for each section, e.g. Hebrews 11: 17-19: Our response to tests reveals how we see God; v. 19: God Provides.

   Hebrews 11:8-10 _____

   Hebrews 11:11-12 _____

   Hebrews 11:13-16 _____

   Hebrews 11:17-19 _____

3. Over and over in the New Testament, God calls Abraham a man of faith. What do these verses say about his faithfulness?

   Romans 4:19-22 _____

   Galatians 3:6 _____

   James 2:23 _____

Practicing Truth in the Family of God

4. The last verse (Heb. 11:19) in this week's study is significant. How does Abraham's ultimate test (Gen. 22) foreshadow Jesus' death and resurrection?

___

When Abraham called the name of the place, "The-LORD-Will-Provide . . . In the Mount of the LORD it shall be provided" (Gen. 22:14), he looked to Calvary, the scene of that grand and awful sacrifice of God's only son, Jesus Christ.

Read John 8:56.
5. Do you think Abraham might have had more understanding than we realize? Why or why not?

___

Challenge Activity: Experience more fully the full grand sweep of Abraham's adventure of faith by reading Genesis 11:27–25:8 in one sitting. Afterwards write a single page description of his faith in your journal.

I LISTEN
How would you describe Abraham if you were given the job of writing his epitaph? (An epitaph is an inscription on a tomb or a short composition in prose or verse, written as a tribute to a dead person.) Review Romans 4:19-22, Galatians 3:6, James 2:23 and Hebrews 11:8,17, then write.

Now do one for yourself. Be adventurous! How do you really want people to remember you?

WE TALK TOGETHER
Talk to God about your dreams, your hopes for the future. Dare to ask Him to give you courage to risk.

WALKING ALONG TOGETHER
When I think of adventure today I think of going to the Holy Land and doing research on a novel about one of the wise men who followed the star. As a child though, adventure meant following the

An Adventure in Faith

creek that flowed through our property. Where did it begin? Where did it end?

Sometimes adventure meant climbing a tall fir tree and turning the branches into a green slide. I'd zip across the needles, land in the soft earth on my bottom and hop up. Another climb, another plunge earthward....

Once my brothers, Dale and Lawrence, were given the job of felling several forty foot fir trees along the fence line. While the saw bit deep into the trunk, Lawrence and I took turns climbing to the top and riding the tree to the ground.

The branches trembled and Lawrence's "timber" shout echoed through the forest as I embraced the trunk. The tree gained momentum as it plunged earthward. At the very last moment I'd let go. When the tree smashed into the dirt, my hands were free. Afterwards I'd pick bits of bark off my shirt and try to peel the pitch off my hands and arms.

An adventure? It seemed so then, but now I'm not so sure.

A Faith That Risks

Even though encountering danger and a liking for excitement is, according to the dictionary definition, part of adventure, there's more. When I place the phrases *to risk, to dare,* and *venture on* alongside Abraham and Sarah, I understand why William Barclay called their lives adventures in faith.

I open my Bible with expectancy. Adventure really does fit with what I'm learning about faith. There's a risk involved with taking God at His Word. Faith really does cause an ordinary life to take on a heavenly sheen; "for he waited for the city which has foundations, whose builder and maker is God" (Heb. 11:10).

Abraham's faith had taken him away from his homeland. Now it's taking him beyond the borders of his tent. Even God's word picture of the starry sky direct his focus away from earth.

I can see him sitting outside his tent, starlight silvering the grass. Is he envisioning the heavenly city God has prepared for him and his family in the distant north? Do his thoughts whisper, *It will be. God has said....*

I know from God's Word that faith that sees every step ahead is not really faith. Yet neither is faith blind. The eyes of faith focus on God's Word. The ears of faith listen to what God has to say. The will of faith

Practicing Truth in the Family of God

obeys, puts a hand to the task, and gets the feet moving in God's direction. I know now that walking by faith makes life an adventure. There's glory in risking everything for our Lord.

A Faith That Waits

Except—even though the moment of decision glows with glory, ordinary days come. Clothes need to be laundered, meals prepared. The office routine needs attention.

I continue to read the passage before me. "And truly if they had called to mind that country from which they had come out, they would have had opportunity to return" (Heb. 11:15).

Opportunity to return? A red light flashes in my brain. I know what returning means. It means quitting. It means going back to where you were at the beginning—perhaps even further back.

I read the verse again, circle the little word *if.* If they had called to mind the place they were before and wanted it badly enough they could have gone back. It's a choice they could have made. A choice that I could make. Except . . . .

I reach for my notebook and begin to write: *Lord, I'm so glad you wrote Abraham's story into this chapter. He didn't quit and I don't have to either. I can keep on because I have Jesus.*

A verse niggles in my mind. Something about looking unto Jesus.

> "Therefore we also, since we are surrounded by so great a cloud of witnesses, let us lay aside every weight, and the sin which so easily ensnares us, and let us run with endurance the race that is set before us, looking unto Jesus the author and finisher of our faith, who for the joy that was set before Him endured the cross, despising the shame, and has sat down on the right hand of the throne of God. For consider Him who endured such hostility from sinners against Himself, lest you become weary and discouraged in your souls" (Heb. 12:1-3).

A Faith That Focuses on Jesus

Sometimes adventuring is a whole lot easier than just plain waiting. Yet it is vision that keeps a man or a woman going. During gray days and cloudy nights, vision looks beyond this world into the face of God. Vision is the stuff that faith is made of.

I write three words in my notebook: *vision, adventure, faith.* These

An Adventure in Faith

three really do fit together. An acrostic follows. It summarizes what God has been teaching me about Abraham in Hebrews 11.

F ocuses on Jesus
A ttentively listens to His Word
I mmediately obeys
T rusts His leading
H opes in His promises

Faith is . . . an adventure with God.

3

Faith for the Family

Hebrews 11:20-29

❦ DAY 1 ❦

GOD SPEAKS

FAITH FOR THE FUTURE

Read Hebrews 11:20-22.
1. Name one thing you would like to communicate to the next generation. Why?

_____

_____

_____

Practicing Truth in the Family of God

2. The ancient patriarchs of these verses are bound together with a common cord. What does the writer of Hebrews say about each one?

   Isaac _____

   Jacob _____

   Joseph _____

Each of these men believed the promises God had made to Abraham. Like Abraham they confessed that they were seeking a heavenly home (Heb. 11:16). Because they were, they had faith for the future. Their faith in God enabled them to have faith for the generations that would come after them.

3. What do you learn about faith from the words these men spoke to various family members at the end of their lives? As you read the following scriptures, note who is speaking, to whom he is speaking, and what he is saying about the future. Include the verse from Hebrews 11:20-22 which corresponds with each account.

   Genesis 27:26-40 _____

   _____

   Genesis 48:9-16 _____

   _____

   Genesis 50:24-26 _____

   _____

Read **Hebrews 11:21** again.
4. Not only did Jacob bless his descendants, he also _____

   _____

Faith for the Family

What more does this teach you about faith?

_____

What effect do you think the memory of Jacob's worship had on his children and his grandchildren?

_____

What is one thing you would like to teach the next generation about worship?

_____

How would you go about teaching it?

_____

A faith that embraces the future, first embraces the heart of God. Only an intimate relationship with God gives us what we need in order to bless others.

Read **Exodus 3:6, Deuteronomy 29:13, 1 Kings 18:36, Acts 7:32.**
5.   Finish the sentence: The LORD is the God of _____, the God of _____, and the God of _____.
If you have trusted Jesus to be your Savior, you can put your name in the following sentence: The LORD is the God of
_____.

I LISTEN
If you were able to write your name in the sentence above, you have something to pass on to future generations. Read Psalm 78:1-7. What are some things you would like to communicate about your faith to those who come after you? What are some practical things you could do that could make this happen?

You might even feel led to write a blessing for a special someone. Begin to pray now about when you should give it to him.

Practicing Truth in the Family of God

WE TALK TOGETHER

Pray for each member of your family or church family by name. Ask God to give you special insight for the needs of each one.

❦ DAY 2 ❦

GOD SPEAKS

A FAMILY THAT BELIEVED GOD'S WORD

Read **Hebrews 11:23.**
1. Have you ever noticed how the coming of a new baby often quickens a parent's faith? Give an example from your own experience or from your own observations.

   _____

Read **Exodus 1.**
2. Give a brief summary of the world Moses was born into.

   _____

Read **Genesis 15:13.**
3. What are the specifics of this promise that God made to Abraham?

   _____

   Why would it have special significance to Moses' parents?

   _____

Read **Exodus 2:1-10** with **Hebrews 11:23.**

We can surmise from these accounts that Moses' parents were led by God to recognize that the unusual beauty of their baby boy meant God had selected him to fulfill the promise made to Abraham 400 years before.

Amram and Jochebed (see Numbers 26:59) chose to trust God rather than to fear Pharoah. When it became impossible for them to

Faith for the Family

hide their baby, they came up with a plan that was both imaginative and resourceful. Together they demonstrated the courage of faith. They even involved their daughter, Miriam.

4. What captures your imagination about this story of this family's faith?

    _____

    How would you like to see faith enacted in your own family?

    _____

    What are one or two practical things you might be able to do that could activate and/or strengthen their faith?

    _____

I LISTEN

Write an imaginary journal entry from the viewpoint of either Amram, Jochebed, Aaron, or Miriam.

It's evening now, the end of a long eventful day. The infant for whom you'd carefully planned is asleep in the corner of a slave's hut. What does God have in mind for this little boy?

Make your entry come alive with specific details. What do you see? hear? smell? What do you feel?

Prayerfully consider reading your entry to your family, especially if you have children. Producing paper and pencils might even inspire them to get in on the fun. Faith and fun served up family style has its reward.

WE TALK TOGETHER

Talk to God about your desire for a family that honors God. Share with Him your dreams, your disappointments, your failures. He loves you. He loves your family.

Practicing Truth in the Family of God

❦ DAY 3 ❦

GOD SPEAKS

MOSES, A MAN WHO FACED A DIFFICULT CHOICE

1. Think about a recent decision you made. What factors influenced you to choose the course of action that you did?

2. Think back over yesterday's study. Write a paragraph contrasting the life of a slave to the life of one who lived in a palace.

Read **Hebrews 11:24-28.**
3. How do these accounts fit in with what you already know about Moses? What additional insights do they give you?

4. List the verbs in Hebrews 11:24-28.

   What do they suggest to you about faith?

5. Jot down the various events the writer of Hebrews chose to illustrate faith in the life of Moses. Why do you think he picked out these particular illustrations?

Faith for the Family

There is a gold mine of truth caught in each of these illustrations. Choose one of them and write down the Old Testament scriptures that refer to that event. (The cross-references in a study Bible will help you.) Compare the account with the phrase in Hebrews that matches them and write down your observations.

<u>Old Testament Scripture</u>　　　　<u>Hebrews 11</u>

Write down three questions from your study. Try to answer at least one of them.

_____

_____

_____

A question many scholars have puzzled over is found in what appears to be a discrepancy between Exodus 2:14 and Hebrews 11:27. How can we synchronize Moses' fear with his faith?

Some commentators think that Moses' forsaking of Egypt refers to the Exodus, but this seems unlikely since it would disrupt the chronological order of the passage. Others think the writer of Hebrews had in mind a different kind of wrath than that occasioned by Moses' killing an Egyptian. Pharoah and his daughter had invested much in their adopted heir. Their hopes for Egypt's future was wrapped up in the skilled statesman and warrior Moses had become.

Moses' rejection of all this must have stirred intense feelings in Pharoah's heart. Hence the wrath in the Exodus account. But Moses persevered. According to Hebrews, his faith in the invisible God enabled him to forsake Egypt's glories.

William Barclay feels there is no real contradiction in these passages. He writes: "For Moses to withdraw to Midian was not an act of

Practicing Truth in the Family of God

fear; it was an act of courage. It showed the courage of the man who has learned to wait."[1]

6. Which of these three ideas seems most reasonable to you? Explain why.

   _____

7. Summarize into one sentence one truth you've discovered about faith from Moses.

   _____

   How would you like to put it into action this week?

   _____

   Tomorrow we'll look more closely at Moses and the Passover.

I LISTEN
Moses knew that God had called him to be the deliverer who would lead his people out of slavery (Acts 7:25). The course he chose was influenced by two factors (Heb. 11:25-26). What were they? What effect could these factors have on decisions you now face or will face in the future?

WE TALK TOGETHER
Ask God to strengthen your faith and give you courage to make decisions based on His Word.

---

1. Barclay, p. 57.

Faith for the Family

❦ DAY 4 ❦

GOD SPEAKS

MOSES AND THE PASSOVER

Read **Hebrews 11:28-29.**
1. Has God ever led you in a direction that didn't make much sense to either you, your family, or your friends? Tell about it.

_____

Read **Exodus 12:5-13.**
2. What is unusual about the instructions God gave Moses?

_____

Read **Exodus 12:14-23.**
3. What kind of picture comes to your mind when you think of Moses, a brilliant and well-educated leader of men, smearing blood on his doorposts?

_____

Do you think you would have been willing to follow his instructions if you had been there? Why or why not?

_____

Read **Exodus 12:14, 24-28.**
Moses demonstrated his faith when He obeyed God's instruction and sacrificed a lamb. His task of leading a nation of slaves into a meaningful celebration of the Passover was also an act of faith. In order to understand its significance to faith, we need to know that the meaning of the Hebrew word translated "Passover," though obscure, probably means, "to pass over by sparing someone." Blood had to be shed by a lamb. That blood had to be applied to the Israelites' homes.

Practicing Truth in the Family of God

4. The festival Moses instituted at this time as a lasting ordinance for the generations to come was to be observed annually. How does this fact alone demonstrate the quality of his faith?

   _____

Read **Exodus 12:29-30** and **Hebrews 11:28.**

When God spared the first-born according to His Word, the Israelites saw that salvation comes from God alone. Although the writer of Hebrews doesn't mention Christ in this verse, he has already pointed to Jesus as the Lamb of God.

His mention of the Passover that ushered in the Last Supper and Christ's death on the cross is in keeping with his great theme that is the heart of God—Jesus is the Shepherd who became the Lamb, the High Priest who becomes the sacrifice.

5. How would you explain this great truth to someone in your family so she could understand?

   _____

Read **Exodus 12:40-42, 51.**

6. How do these verses increase your own faith in God's faithfulness?

   _____

7. What is the source of the great faith that enabled Moses to follow God's instructions even when they didn't make much sense? The following scriptures give insight:

   Hebrews 11:27 _____

   Exodus 33:9-11 _____

   Numbers 12:7-8 _____

Faith for the Family

I LISTEN

What one or two things could you do that would help you get to know God more intimately? Explore your thoughts in your journal as you ask Him to give you direction and creative ideas.

WE TALK TOGETHER

Ask God to give you understanding in how you can communicate the truth of His Word to the next generation.

❦ DAY 5 ❦

GOD SPEAKS

THE CROSSING OF THE RED SEA

Read **Hebrews 11:29.**
1. What kind of picture does the word *miracle* bring to your mind?

   _____

2. To whom is the writer referring to in this verse?

   _____

   Contrast is effectively used two times in the one sentence in this verse. Notice how it paints a forceful and forever picture of the miracle of Exodus 14. The Red Sea is contrasted with _____ _____, the Israelites _____ with the Egyptians who _____.
   Drawing a simple sketch of these events will etch it even more firmly into your mind and heart.

Practicing Truth in the Family of God

3. Together Moses and the Israelites with whom he identified accomplished the impossible. What are some things that a group of believers, united in faith, can accomplish that one person alone cannot?

___

Read **Exodus 14.**

4. What encouragement does it give you to realize that the Israelites who, "by faith," walked through the Red Sea had fears and doubts and complaints—just like we do?

___

5. What does God's response to their cries tell you about God?

___

I LISTEN

Exodus 15 is the song Moses and Miriam sang after God brought them safely across the Red Sea. Note verses 11-13. Paraphrase them into your own song of praise.

WE SING TOGETHER

Sing your song of praise to your Lord.

Challenge Activity: Read the following verses in Hebrews 11 and complete a "by faith" sentence with a "faith truth" you discovered this week. The first one is done for you.

vv. 20-22: By faith we look to God to fulfill His promises to future generations.

v. 23: By faith ___

___

v. 24: By faith ___

___

Faith for the Family

vv. 25-26: By faith _____

_____

v. 27: By faith _____

_____

v. 28: By faith _____

_____

v. 29: By faith _____

_____

WALKING ALONG TOGETHER

The phone rang this morning. It was my mother. "Aunt Aggie has pneumonia," she said. "Dean doesn't think she'll live much longer."

Aunt Aggie. We've known for some time now that she's getting ready to go home to be with Jesus.

Aunt Aggie. Memory stabs me. Six boys—cousins; two were my brothers, the other four, Aggie's boys.

Sometimes my mother and aunt got together and talked about their boys. They did more than talk to each other though. They talked to God.

It seems God had given each of these mothers an unusual assurance that God would use their youngest sons in a special way in His service. Except—the years passed. My brother, Dale, and Aunt Aggie's oldest son continued in what they had been taught from God's Word. Her two middle sons preached and taught. But her youngest son, Danny, and my brother, Lawrence—the two the mothers had prayed so fervently would be used by God in a special way—chose other directions.

One day my mother and I talked about it.

A Mother's Prayers

"Sometimes I wonder about the prayers Aggie and I prayed for Lawrence and Danny. We had such faith—and yet—could it be that

Practicing Truth in the Family of God

God pressed those two boys on our hearts the way He did because He knew they'd make choices that would lead them away from God's best for them?

"They were so close to God when they were little. We had such dreams for them."

I put my arm around her shoulders. "I don't know, Mother. So many things I don't understand."

I reached for my Bible. I needed to show Mother the verse God had given me years before. "Listen, here's a promise God gave me from Isaiah 54:13 when my kids were little: '*All* thy children shall be taught of the Lord, and great shall be the peace of thy children' (KJV). *All* — no if or excepts or buts. Just *all*. But sometimes my faith wavers. My son, Dow, is one of those children. He's 35 and he still hasn't turned back to the Lord."

"Lawrence and Danny are in their fifties."

"Abraham and Sarah waited 25 years before Isaac was born. Even though God promised them they'd possess the land, they never did have a place to call home. Abraham even had to buy a burial plot for Sarah in the very place God promised to give him."

From My Journal

Lord, there's so many things about faith I don't understand. A letter from my friend, Jan—her daughter's dead—a head on collision and her daughter had been drinking. And how Jan prayed for her girl.

Lord, I don't like it when my doubts mount up, rising higher and higher. Oh, I know You're faithful to Your Word. I can recount the times I stood on Your promises. When I prayed and You burst forth in action. Why, You brought my own daughter, Beth, back to us when she was wandering so far away.

But the other times are there, too. White nights when the heavens seemed like brass and I didn't understand. I still don't.

Thoughts from Him

That night a verse wings into my thoughts. "Faith, hope, love, these three. But the greatest of these is love."

I turn on the light and reach for my Amplified Bible. I find the verse I'm looking for in 1 Corinthians 13, the love chapter: "And so faith, hope, love abide; [faith, conviction and belief respecting a man's relation to God and divine things; hope, joyful and confident

Faith for the Family

expectation of eternal salvation; love, true affection for God and man, growing out of God's love for and in us], these three, but the greatest of these is love" (v. 13).

In the morning I waken with a thought: *Faith is the result of love. When my love for my Lord grows, my faith grows.*

I open my journal and write: *Love is the power, faith the action. Faith results from love and becomes an ever-increasing stream that flows from the heart of God. That stream propels me to act, to do, to love the things my Lord loves."*

I sketch a stream flowing from a heart. The stick figure walking on the stream is me.

Underneath I write: *But I can't walk on water! Oh, yes, I can! I can! I can do all things through Him who loves me.*

My steps seems to echo back my thoughts as I go down the stairs. "Faith results from love.

"Lord, I love you so much.

"Faith results from love."

Suddenly I know. The entire book of Hebrews abounds in love. The Shepherd who became the Lamb is a manifestation of that love in action. He is the source of faith.

"Lord, if I could teach my children and grandchildren just one things it would be that You love them."

Just Let Me Love You

That night I write the words my Lord pressed into my heart throughout the day.

"Eva, you want to grow in faith? Then just let Me love you—freely—gently, for MY Name's sake.

"As I love you, your heart will warm, your faith increase. You will mount up with wings like an eagle. You will run and not be weary, you will walk and not faint.

"Wait on Me and I will strengthen your heart."

I write my response back to Him: *Lord, I'm waiting. Aunt Aggie's waiting, too. It won't be long now and she'll mount up with wings as an eagle. She'll enter that heavenly city Abraham saw from afar. She'll see you face to face.*

Someday, Danny and Lawrence will be there, too (Rev. 22:3-4). *They will see your face. They will serve you. The unseen will be reality.*

Practicing Truth in the Family of God

My son's face floats before my eyes. *"Lord, my deepest need right now is faith for my family—my son. Faith, hope, love—these three...*.

"As my love grows, my faith will increase."

4

A Faith That Endures

Hebrews 11:30-40

❦ DAY 1 ❦

GOD SPEAKS

A FAITH THAT BREAKS DOWN WALLS

1. At one time or another we all face situations that seem impossible to handle. Circle the one you most identify with:
   a severed relationship
   a colicky baby
   an incompetent secretary
   a boss who harasses you
   a rebellious family member
   unemployment
   Other: _____

Practicing Truth in the Family of God

Read Hebrews 11:30-31 and Joshua 6:1-20.

Forty years have passed since Israel, because of unbelief, refused to enter Canaan, the Promised Land. But now their sons and daughters, in direct contrast to these who went before, trust God.

Jericho was strategically located. Although the heavily-walled city was comparatively small, it was filled with mighty warriors who prevented invaders from entering the valleys that led to the central part of Canaan.

2. The writer of Hebrews doesn't say by whose faith the walls of Jericho fell down. According to the account in Joshua, who believed God's promise and obeyed His instructions?

   _____

3. Write down your observations on the following. Include a verse or verses with each one:

   God's promise: _____

   God's instructions: _____

   Joshua's instructions: _____

   The people's response: _____

   The result of faith: _____

God often gives His people promises concerning certain persons and/or situations. However the fulfillment of the promise often requires that a certain condition be met.

Read Joshua 6:2-5.
4. Write down God's promise, the people's responsibility, and the results that would follow if they obeyed His Word in the spaces below.

His Promise	What the people must do	Results
_____	_____	_____

A Faith That Endures

5. Has God given you a special promise in His Word concerning a certain person or situation? What is it?

   _____

   Use the lines below to clarify what God wants to do and what your responsibility is.

His Promise	What I must do	Results
_____	_____	_____

   What does this show you about faith?

   _____

6. In our previous study, *Getting to Know the Heart of God*, we discovered that the ark of the covenant symbolized God's presence. How many times is it mentioned in Joshua 6:1-20? _____ How do you think this visual reminder strengthened the people's faith?

   _____

   How does it strengthen your faith? (See Hebrews 13:5-6.)

   _____

I LISTEN

Are you facing an impossible wall right now? Perhaps a task that's far beyond your capabilities? Or a different kind of obstacle? A pain that won't go away? A habit that has enslaved you? Whatever it is you can know that God specializes in tearing down walls.

Explore a wall in your life in your journal. Ask God to show you in His Word what He wants to do. Ask Him what He wants you to do.

WE TALK TOGETHER

Ask Him to reveal to you His specific battle plan for breaking down your wall. Partner together with Him as you surround it with prayer and faith.

Practicing Truth in the Family of God

❦ DAY 2 ❦

GOD SPEAKS

A WOMAN OF FAITH

Read **Hebrews 11:31.**
1. Have you ever felt you would never be able to live triumphantly because of something in your past? Tell about it.

_____

_____

Earlier the writer to the Hebrews wrote about the Israelites who perished in the desert (Heb. 3:17). Now he uses the same word, *disobedient*, to describe the inhabitants of Jericho. His purpose: to contrast the obedience of one woman with the disobedience of a nation.

2. Who is Rahab? What do you remember about her?

_____

Read **Joshua 2:1-21, 6:21-25.**

In the midst of Jericho's walls' crashing down, it would be easy to miss this less conspicuous miracle. Describe what happened to Rahab's home which sat on top of Jericho's wall (Josh. 2:15; 6:20, 22).

3. What happened to her family?

_____

4. The Hebrew word for *harlot* in these verses is not that of a temple prostitute but of a secular prostitute. How does it make you feel to realize that this woman who had been involved in sinful prostitution was spared because of her faith in God?

A Faith That Endures

_____

Read Rahab's testimony again (Josh. 2:9-13).

5. What does Rahab know about God?

_____

What did her understanding of Him enable her to do?

_____

It is extraordinary that Rahab, a Gentile and a prostitute, made such a mark on Israel. Even the rabbis were proud to trace their ancestry to this remarkable woman of faith. The writer of Hebrews also included her in the faith chapter.

6. What do other New Testament writers say about her?

   Matthew 1:5 _____

   James 2:25 _____

Rahab had three strikes against her. She was a pagan Canaanite, a prostitute, and a woman. But even though the men in Israel were the heirs of God's promise, when it came to faith, there were no distinctions (Gal. 3:28-29). When she and her family walked away from Jericho they walked into a new life.

7. Complete the following sentences: Because of her faith, Rahab was accepted by the _____.
   She married _____,
   became the mother of _____,
   who was great-grandfather of _____.

I LISTEN

God never intended that a sinful past keep anyone from experiencing a triumphant faith. Not only does He cleanse and purify our

Practicing Truth in the Family of God

hearts, He wants to restore our self-worth in our own eyes. He wants to restore it in the eyes of the world.

Take time right now and create a character sketch of the woman you want to be. When you've finished, write "BY FAITH" across your word picture. Underneath write one action step you can take today to help you develop spiritual maturity.

WE TALK TOGETHER

Unbelief results in disobedience; faith results in obedience. Pray that you and your family will walk in obedience to God's Word today.

❦ DAY 3 ❦

GOD SPEAKS

THOSE WHO CONQUERED THROUGH FAITH

Read **Hebrews 11:32-35.**

Scholars have been quick to point out that four of the men in the list in verse 32 had definite shortcomings. Leon Morris quotes from Calvin: "In every saint there is always to be found something reprehensible. Nevertheless although faith may be imperfect and incomplete it does not cease to be approved by God." (in loc.).[1]

1. Does this statement encourage or discourage you in your quest to grow in faith? What is your reaction?

The theme of Hebrews 11 is endurance by faith—it demonstrates what faith looks like in the lives of ordinary people—people who struggled, who sometimes failed, but who kept on going with God. Earlier the writer named specific individuals and their "faith" experiences. Now he mentions several more people without describing their

---

1. Leon Morris, *The Expositor's Bible Commentary* (Grand Rapids, MI: The Zondervan Corporation, 1981), p. 130.

A Faith That Endures

experiences.

2. What pronoun does the writer use for the first time in the rhetorical question in verse 32? Why do you think he does it here?

   _____

3. The same reason the writer cannot now list the many examples of faith is the same reason why we cannot now study each of these individuals in detail. Who are these people of faith? Put an asterisk beside the name or names of those whose faith has been most memorable to you.

   _____

   Add the names of people you think would be included if the list were continued today. Be ready to explain why you chose them.

   _____

   _____

The writer next summarizes categories of deeds of faith (vv. 33-35). Instead of names, phrases particularly suited to stir the memories of readers have been selected.

4. List these phrases in the form of a question. Answer as many as you can with the name/or names they suggest to you. The first two are done for you.
   Helpful Hint: Don't expect your list to look like someone else's. Allow the Holy Spirit to bring to your mind the ones most needful for your own faith building right now.

   Who through faith subdued kingdoms? Joshua

   Who worked righteousness? Samuel and Solomon

   _____

Practicing Truth in the Family of God

_____

_____

_____

_____

5. A character study of a Bible character can add richness to your personal study of God's Word. Choose a name from today's study and try to answer the questions below. A Study Bible with cross-references, a concordance, and/or a Bible dictionary can help you find the verses you need. Include the scripture references with each discovery.

Who? _____

What? _____

Where? _____

When? _____

Why? _____

How? _____

How does _____ see God?

I LISTEN

The writer doesn't tell his readers what they are to remember. Instead he inspires them to draw upon their own treasure of scriptural knowledge.

What is God just now calling you to remember? How does your particular memory strengthen your faith?

A Faith That Endures

WE TALK TOGETHER

Ask God how you might emulate the faith of the person you selected to study more in depth. Thank God for teaching you more about what it means to live by faith.

❦ DAY 4 ❦

GOD SPEAKS

THE TRAGEDIES OF FAITH

1. How do you feel when "bad things happen to good people"? What questions do you ask? What kind of statements do you make?

   _____

   _____

At the beginning of the chapter we saw blessings resulting from faith. Now hardships come into focus. *The International Bible Commentary,* edited by F.F. Bruce, calls this (vv. 29-38) one of the most beautiful passages in Hebrews.

> It serves magnificently to summarize the writer's concept of faith. It is that which drives one forward always, never allowing the luxury of retreat. It is "venturesome action." It is trust and confidence. It is obedience. It is endurance. Faith is seeing the invisible in clear focus.[2]

Read **Hebrews 11:35-38.**
2. Who are these unnamed believers, the others who suffered tragedy because of their faith? Let's find out.

   List the verbs in 35-38: _____

---

2. *The International Bible Commentary* (Carmel, NY: Guideposts, 1979), p. 1528.

Practicing Truth in the Family of God

    List the nouns: _____

    List the adjectives: _____

3. Continue reading to the end of the chapter. How would you describe the mood of this passage in a single phrase or sentence (Heb. 11:35-40)?

_____

Although no one is mentioned by name we can, by searching the scriptures, discover who some of these people probably were.

4. Who suffered from mockings and scourgings, chains and imprisonments (v. 36)?

1 Kings 22:24: _____

Jeremiah 20:2; 37:15; 38:6: _____

Who was stoned to death because of his faith (v. 37)?

2 Chronicles 24:20-21 with **Matthew 23:35:** _____

_____

Who were slain with the sword (v. 37)?

Jeremiah 26:20-23: _____

Acts 12:2: _____

Who went about in sheepskins and goatskins, destitute, afflicted and tormented; wandering in deserts and mountains, in dens and caves (vv. 37-38)?

2 Kings 1:7: _____

1 Kings 18:4, 13; 19:9: _____

A Faith That Endures

Although the Old Testament doesn't give an account of a person being tortured (v. 35) and refusing deliverance (the Greek word for *torture* is to be stretched on the rack and beaten to death), this did happen during Maccabean times (approx. 168-165 B.C.). A man named Eleazar accepted the horrors of an awful death rather than deny His Lord. His martyrdom is recorded in 2 Macabees and is followed by the account of a mother and seven sons. One after another these men endured horrible torture rather than deny God. Their mother encouraged them by affirming that there would be a future resurrection.

5. What one word would you use to describe this mother's faith?

___

Nowhere in Scripture do we find anyone who was "sawn in two." However, both Jewish and Christian tradition say that the prophet Isaiah, during the reign of the wicked King Manasseh, was seized in the Judean hill country. He was sawn in two with a wooden saw.

6. Compare **Daniel 11:33** with **Hebrews 11:38**. What further insight do these verses give you concerning faith and suffering?

___

How does the writer of Hebrews summarize the courageous faith of these suffering saints?

___

I LISTEN

The early church considered those who suffered in the Maccabbean days as the "greatest martyrs before the martyrs."

Augustine wrote, "They could not confess Christ openly, for the name of Christ was not yet revealed; yet they died for the name of Christ veiled in the Law."

Allow your heart to respond to the recognition that you know the name of the One these Old Testament martyrs had not yet seen, the Promised Messiah, whom they were willing to die for.

Practicing Truth in the Family of God

I WORSHIP HIM

Find the hymn, *Am I A Soldier of the Cross?* by Isaac Watts. Meditate on the words. Talk to your Lord about faith and hard times.

🌿 DAY 5 🌿

GOD SPEAKS

SOMETHING BETTER

1. What does it mean to you to know that you have the approval of those closest to you?

   _____

   Have you ever experienced a time when you knew your family or friends didn't approve of you? What effect did their disapproval have?

   _____

Read **Hebrews 11:39-40.**

These last two verses radiate God's approval of those who lived—and died—by faith. Read these verses in as many different translations as possible. For example the NIV Bible says, "These were all commended for their faith, yet none of them received what had been promised. God has planned something better for us so that only together with us would they be made perfect."

The Amplified Bible says, "And all of these, though they won divine approval by [means of] their faith, did not receive the fulfillment of what was promised. Because God had us in mind and had something better and greater in view for us, so that they [these heroes and heroines of faith] should not come to perfection apart from us, [that is, before we could join them]."

2. What insights did you gain from reading the different translations?

   _____

A Faith That Endures

3. According to verse 39, what reward did these saints of whom "the world was not worthy" (v. 38) receive?

_____

Read 1 Peter 1:10-11 and Hebrews 11:40.

4. What did these Old Testament believers not receive?

_____

5. The writer of Hebrews ends that chapter by including his readers. And that includes us. What is the "something better" we and these heroes of faith share together?

_____

Only Christ's work on the cross could bring Old Testament saints, New Testament saints, and the saints of today into the presence of God. We are together one family and "a family is not complete unless all its members are present."[3]

6. How does God's bringing "us" Christians today into His ultimate plan make you feel?

_____

William Barclay in *The Letter to the Hebrews* has this to say about these last verses in the faith chapter:

> In the end he says a great thing. All these died before the final unfolding of God's promise and the coming of the Messiah into the world. It was as if God had so arranged things that the full blaze of his glory should not be revealed until we and they can enjoy it together. The writer to the Hebrews is saying: "See! the glory of God has come. But see what it cost to enable it to come!

---

3. Hugh Montefiore, *The Epistle to the Hebrews* (New York and Evanston: Harper and Row, 1964), p. 212.

Practicing Truth in the Family of God

That is the faith which gave you your religion. What can you do but be true to a heritage like that![4]

Reread **Hebrews 11**.

7. What evidences of faith have you been able to see working in your life since you first began this study?

_____

What effect has it had on your family and friends?

_____

I LISTEN

Read Hebrews 12:1-2. The long list of heroes is referred to here as a "cloud of witnesses." The writer then points to Jesus.

Draw clouds in your journal. Label them with the names of the Old Testament saints you've studied these past few weeks. Draw a cross in the midst of the clouds. Underneath write: Look to Jesus.

I WORSHIP HIM

Direct your praises to Jesus who is the Author and Finisher of your faith. In Him and Him alone does faith find perfect expression.

Challenge Activity: With the help of a concordance, find and read as many "faith" verses as you can. Choose one of them to memorize this week.

WALKING ALONG TOGETHER

"You write about spiritual maturity but I see no evidence of it in your life." Although these words were spoken to me by a man who'd only known me for a few months, he was presently one of my spiritual leaders.

His words cut into the very depths of who I was. My faith trembled as others seemed to believe his perception of me. Except for my family and a few close friends, I felt totally misunderstood.

Then abandoned.

---

4. Barclay, p. 171.

A Faith That Endures

How was I going to endure? Would I ever be able to teach again? to write?

As darkness and loneliness closed in around me, I found it hard to pray or read my Bible.

Then an article surfaced. I have no idea why I'd saved it, but there in a box of clippings was, *"Taking God at His Word"* by Theodore H. Epp.

A sentence was underlined in red: "If there is to be Christian maturity there must be faith in God's Word and an obedience to what it says."[5]

Other sentences caught my attention.

"God actually speaks to believers through His Word as they read it."[6]

"God's word is the basis of spiritual maturity."[7]

"Faith is the principle by which God works in each individual."[8]

"'So then faith comes by hearing, and hearing by the Word of God' (Rom. 10:17)."[9]

A Childhood Memory

I've known Romans 10:17 since I was a little girl. Bible stories are wrapped around it.

Unable to attend Sunday school and church, my mother decided to teach us three kids and the Blackwell kids who lived down the road stories from the Bible.

Mother didn't just tell us the stories. She got us involved. I'm not sure what we constructed the walls of Jericho out of, but I do remember strewing real straw on the roof of Rahab's house. That straw represented the stalks of flax in which she hid the spies.

The bright red material I braided into a cord and let down the wall fascinated me. As little as I was, I understood that the red cord pointed to the cross of Jesus and the blood He shed for me.

"It was Rahab's faith in the words God spoke that saved her and

---

5. Theodore H. Epp, "Taking God at His Word." *The Good News Broadcaster*, October 1976.
6. Ibid.
7. Ibid.
8. Ibid.
9. Ibid.

Practicing Truth in the Family of God

her family," my mother explained. "When you listen to Bible stories, you're hearing God's Word. Your faith begins to grow."

I'm not sure what else Mother said. Something about, "Rahab didn't know a lot about God, but what she knew was enough for her to risk her life for." I do know the walls made a glorious crash when we pushed them over.

Consider God's Words

Epp's words followed me into my day. "God actually speaks to believers through His Word as they read it. Faith is the principle by which God works in each individual. So then, 'faith comes by hearing, and hearing by the Word of God.'"[10]

I knew these words were true. That night I curled up on the couch with my Bible. "Lord, what did Rahab know about you?"

I read her words in Joshua: "The Lord your God, He is God in heaven above and on earth beneath" (Josh. 2:11).

These words were from the Lord. Moses, the man who spoke with God face to face, had said them in Deuteronomy 4:39: "Therefore know this day, and consider it in your heart, that the LORD Himself is God in heaven above and on the earth beneath; there is no other."

No, there is no other. And this God who is above all and beneath all is the One who has given me everything I need for life and godliness.

Everything I need.

I turn the pages of my Bible. The verse I'm looking for is in 2 Peter: "His divine power has given us everything we need for life and godliness through our knowledge of him who called us by his own glory and goodness" (2 Pet. 1:3 NIV).

God is calling me. I'm ready to return to my study in Hebrews.

I start with Hebrews 10:32 and keep reading. The faith of Abel and Noah and Enoch. Abraham, Isaac and Jacob. The faith of Moses and Rahab.

I reach for my journal and begin to write: *Faith is action. Faith is believing. Faith is triumphant.*

Lord, I haven't conquered kingdoms, shut the mouths of lions or quenched fires. But Lord, you're turning my weakness into strength.

When I come to the phrase, "women receive back their dead, raised to life again," tears come. *Lord, I know what it's like to see the death*

---

10. Epp.

A Faith That Endures

of a dream and even that of relationships that were so precious. But You are the God of resurrection. You have power to bring life out of death. You, Yourself, are everything I need.

I sketch a gift box with a bow in the margin, label it, *"EVERYTHING I NEED."* Underneath I write: *Faith accepts the gift that even now gives growing power.*

I can go on to spiritual maturity.

5

Running the Race

Hebrews 12:1-13

❦ DAY 1 ❦

GOD SPEAKS

THE RACE

1. What are some things you'd do if you were about to participate in a cross-country race?

   _____

Read **Hebrews 12:1-2**.
2. How does the "Therefore" in verse 1 tie Hebrews 11 and 12 together?

   _____

Practicing Truth in the Family of God

In these verses, the writer of Hebrews uses the race as a metaphor of the Christian life. But the "witnesses" are more than mere spectators. (The Greek word translated is the origin of the English word "martyr" and means "testifiers" or "witnesses.") The lives of the men and woman in Hebrews 11 were testimonies to faith's power. Their lives encourage us to "run the race" and cross the finish line.

Write down your own observations from these verses.

_____

_____

3. These verses give specific instructions in how to run successfully. The first deals with preparation. What two things are we to do to prepare for the race (v. 1)?

_____

What are some things that are not wrong in themselves but hinder us from our best efforts?

_____

The context of Hebrews suggests that the sin mentioned here is that of unbelief. How has this particular sin ensnared you?

_____

What does God ask you to do with these weights and sins?

_____

4. *Endurance* and *endure* are important words in this chapter. Look them up in your dictionary. Write down phrases that help you better understand their meaning.

_____

Running the Race

William Barclay describes endurance as "a determination, unhurrying and yet undelaying, which goes steadily on and refuses to be deflected," and "the steadfast endurance which carries on until in the end it gets there."[1] Later he describes a Greek athlete who flings himself on the ground, only *after* he has passed the finish line.

5. The apostle Paul also uses the theme of the race to teach spiritual truth. Write down your observations from the following scriptures.

    1 Corinthians 9:24-27 _____

    2 Timothy 2:5 _____

Read **Hebrews 12:2** again.

6. This verse gives specific instructions on our running style. Finish the sentence: We are to keep our heads up and _____ (v. 2).

    This verse calls Jesus the _____ and _____ of our _____.

    On what did Jesus fix His gaze?

    _____

The Expositor's Bible Commentary makes this statement: "He looked right through the Cross to the coming joy, the joy of bringing salvation to those he loves."[2] Jesus completed his work of redemption when He sat down at the right hand of the throne of God. He finished the race.

How does this verse encourage you to keep running?

_____

---

1. Barclay, pp. 173-174.
2. *The Expositor's Bible Commentary*, p. 134.

Practicing Truth in the Family of God

I LISTEN

Jesus is our ultimate example of faithfulness. The heroes of faith challenge and encourage us but Jesus does what no person can do. He gives us His Spirit who empowers us to endure. Read Zechariah 4:6-7 and Isaiah 40:29-31. Choose one of these verses and paraphrase it into your own words.

WE TALK TOGETHER

Ask God to help you, "strip off anything that slows you down or holds you back, and especially those sins that wrap themselves so tightly around your feet and trip you up; and run with patience the particular race that God has set before you" (paraphrased from Hebrews 12:1 of the TLB).

❦ DAY 2 ❦

GOD SPEAKS

CONSIDER JESUS

Read **Hebrews 12:1-4**.
1. What are some things that make you weary?

_____

What has power to discourage you?

_____

The two verbs (translated "grow weary" and "lose heart" in the NIV) at the end of verse 3 were used by Aristotle of runners who relaxed and collapsed after they passed the finishing post.

2. What is the antidote for the weariness expressed here?

_____

When the writer instructs his readers to "consider Jesus" he's

Running the Race

telling them to look intently at Him. Although the writer seldom directly alludes to Jesus' earthly life, he does so here; it is his only mention of the cross in the letter to the Hebrews.

Read **Mark 15:15-40**.
3. Compare what makes you weary and ready to lose heart to what Jesus faced when He went to the cross. What do you discover?

_____

Read **Luke 22:61-62.**
How did Peter's look into the face of Jesus before Jesus went to the cross affect him?

_____

Read **Acts 7:55-56.**
Stephen also demonstrated the power of looking intently into the face of Jesus.

What does he see? What does his steadfast gaze teach you?

_____

_____

Read **Hebrews 12:4** again.
4. What does the writer remind his readers of?

_____

What gentle reprimand is there for you in this verse?

_____

How does it encourage you to keep on in the race?

_____

Practicing Truth in the Family of God

I LISTEN

That Jesus is even now at the Father's right hand in heaven should have a profound effect on the way we run the race. Review Hebrews 4:14-16. What do these verses encourage you to do?

WE TALK TOGETHER

The goal of the Christian should be to grow in Christ likeness. We can only do that by looking unto Jesus. Ask the Holy Spirit to help you focus on the Son right now.

🐞 DAY 3 🐞

GOD SPEAKS

A FORGOTTEN WORD OF ENCOURAGEMENT

1. Proverbs are short terse sayings that give practical instruction on the art of living. Write down one that is significant to you.

   _____

Read **Hebrews 12:5-6**.
2. What had these believers forgotten?

   _____

The early believers often memorized passages from the Old Testament when they attended worship services. The writer of Hebrews here refers to a proverb that was basic training to the believers in the church.

3. Earlier he had rebuked his readers for being slow to learn (Heb. 5:11). How does this tie together with what he's telling them now?

   _____

Read **Proverbs 3:11-12**. Compare with **Hebrews 12:5-6**.

Running the Race

The writer of Hebrews uses this proverb to illustrate two negative reactions people can fall into when they are being disciplined by the Lord. Both of these can cause shipwreck.

4. What are they?

   (Hebrews 5a) _____

   (Hebrews 5b) _____

5. Proverbs 3:12 and Hebrews 5:6 help us put the suffering we experience at the hand of our heavenly Father into a right perspective. What two things do we need to remember?

   1. _____

   2. _____

It helps to compare the suffering brought about by the sinful things done against believers to force them to abandon their faith with the suffering we experience as a child of God. The world purposes to destroy our faith. The Father disciplines us for the purpose of transforming our character.

6. Which warning from Hebrews 12:5 and Proverbs 3:11 is most applicable for you today?

   _____

   What word of encouragement from Hebrews 12:6 and Proverbs 3:12 is most meaningful?

   _____

I LISTEN

Paraphrase Proverbs 3:11-12 into your own words. It may be helpful to change "My son" to "My daughter."

Practicing Truth in the Family of God

WE TALK TOGETHER

Thank the Father for making you His daughter. Ask Him to show you something you can do to delight His Father heart. Then do it!

❦ DAY 4 ❦

GOD SPEAKS

GOD'S DISCIPLINE

Read **Hebrews 12:5-11**.
1. What is your reaction to these words?

   exhortation _____

   chastening _____

   rebuked _____

   scourges _____

   subjection _____

2. Read these verses in Hebrews in as many translations as you can.

   chastening? _____

   rebuked? _____

   scourges? _____

   subjection? _____

   What further insights did you discover?

   _____

Running the Race

What other words did you find used for exhortation?

_____

3. There are four principles from Hebrews 12:7-11 that will help us endure when we are being disciplined. Prayerfully read these verses and finish the sentences as best you can. Additional scriptures have been given to help you.

Principle 1 (vv. 7-8): Discipline assures us that _____

_____ (Gal. 4:6-7).

Principle 2 (v. 9): Discipline deepens the quality of our _____
_____ (Prov. 6:23, 10:16-17).

Principle 3 (v.10): Discipline is for our _____
(Rom. 8:28).

Principle 4 (v. 11): Discipline, though painful, brings _____
_____ (John 15:1-2).

I LISTEN

God's training doesn't end when we grow up. It lasts all our lives. Use the principles in today's lesson to examine your own attitude toward His discipline. What do you think He wants to teach you right now?

WE TALK TOGETHER

Talk to your heavenly Father about some of the hard things you've experienced since you've begun to serve Him. Ask Him to help you patiently and expectantly wait for the peaceful fruit of righteousness that He desires to produce in you.

Practicing Truth in the Family of God

❦ DAY 5 ❦

GOD SPEAKS

STRENGTHENING THE WEAK

1. Can you think of a time when you responded correctly to the Lord's discipline in your life? Tell about it.

   _____

   What effect did it have on those around you?

   _____

   Read **Hebrews 12:12-13**.
   "Therefore" in verse 12 links this exhortation to God's discipline. Read these verses in several translations. For example, the NIV says: "Therefore, strengthen your feeble arms and weak knees. 'Make level paths for your feet,' so that the lame may not be disabled, but rather healed."

2. The picture here is of someone who has been out of action but who is now told to put things right and get moving. Have you ever been so weakened spiritually that you felt paralyzed, unable to help another? Tell about it.

   _____

   _____

   According to these verses, what should come as a result of God's discipline in your life?

   _____

   In the lives of others?

Running the Race

Discipline makes us spiritually whole so that we can run the race with endurance. A healthy member of the Body runs in such a way that those who are weak (lame) are strengthened.

3. Earlier the writer of Hebrews urged his readers to take their responsiblity to others seriously (Heb. 3:13, 4:1, 11, 6:11). What kind of care are we to give others in the Body?

Galatians 6:1-2 _____

Ephesians 4:15-16 _____

1 Thessalonians 5:14 _____

Hebrews 13:3 _____

I LISTEN

The writer of Hebrews talks to his team like a coach in Hebrews 12:12-13. He knows his runners are tired: "Strengthen your feeble hands and weak knees." He knows they need instruction: "Make level paths for your feet."

Ask God to bring to your mind someone in the race of life who is in some way spiritually handicapped. How can you encourage her to keep running?

WE TALK TOGETHER

William Barclay writes, "One of life's greatest glories is to be an encourager of the man who is near to despair and a strengthener of the man whose strength is failing."[4]

Ask God to make you into an encourager of others.

Challenge Activity: Make a list of obstacles that impede your progress and the progress of others in the race of life. (It may be a political issue or something that has a negative effect on the children

---

4. Barclay, p. 180.

Practicing Truth in the Family of God

in your church or community.) Choose one and develop a plan that will help remove it. Ask God to give you insight as you think it through with Him.

WALKING ALONG TOGETHER
Run . . . endure . . . agonize . . . persevere . . .

The race track stretches before me and I have to run. It's a command—run with patience the race set before you. Except it isn't ahead of me. It's all around me and I feel like I've been running for a long, long time.

And not just running. I've soared. I've stumbled. I've fallen. Most of all, I've plodded—one step at a time.

Hot Sunshine and Cool Shade

A memory—I'm nine years old and my brothers and I have a job picking strawberries at the neighbor's place a mile down the road and then another quarter or so after the crossroads. We have to walk to get there but it doesn't matter. At least it didn't at first. The morning is cool and there's a certain excitement as we talk about the money we'll earn. The neighbor said he'd pay us twenty-five cents for every carrier we picked and we could hardly wait. Except the sun shone hot and the day stretched long. At 2 o'clock I stuffed a single dollar into my pocket and headed for home.

The details of that walk are still vivid. The boys took off ahead of me and I plodded along alone. A long stretch of road bordered by fields meant sunshine all the way. But there was a huge oak alongside the road that offered a slight reprieve. After that, more sunshine, and then a wooded area where sheep grazed. I fixed my eyes on the dense shade cast by the fir trees and ploded on.

After that, more sunshine, and then the trees along our driveway welcomed me. My knees trembled by this time, and my face felt like it was on fire.

But I kept going.

I opened the door and stepped inside. My eye caught my reflection in the mirror in the front room. I couldn't tell where the red strawberry juice around my mouth ended and the sunburn on my cheeks began.

But I had made it. I stepped across the threshold.

I was home.

Running the Race

A Page from an Old Journal

Another memory. This one was wrapped inside a cardboard box squashed inside a closet. When I opened it I found a baby's faded yellow gown.

I found something else—a page from an old journal I'd written during the time my home overflowed with children.

As I read, I could tell that I was in the race of life—the very thick of it, and I was tired, so very, very tired. I have no idea whether or not I knew about the race when I wrote it.

But I was running. I was doing something the writer of Hebrews had instructed his readers to do—I was looking unto Jesus.

I was using God's Word to focus on my Lord.

Psalms 5, a Mother's Paraphrase

Lord, please, listen carefully to me. Please pay attention. I need someone to listen, to carefully weigh what I say.

Hear the sound of my voice. Please pay attention when I cry a little, for You are my King, the majestic One whom I long to have rule my life.

You are going to hear me in the morning, Lord. Right in the middle of breakfast confusion I'm going to direct my prayer to You.

Lord, Darren is kicking Mark. I need your firmness now. Beth's stomach hurts. Is it a school problem? I need Your wisdom now.

Yes, Lord, in the morning I will look up. After the older children are gone and before the little ones are awake I will look into Your face.

For a little while I won't look around me or even within me. I will simply enjoy Your presence and thank You for loving me.

When I look at You, I see Your beauty. You are my Father, the One who disciplines me for my own good and for the good of my children. You are the one who lifts up my head....

Only one page. It is enough.

Remembering Again

Later that day, I wrote a page in my 1994 journal.

Lord, You were with me when I was a little girl with strawberries on my face, plodding home in the heat. You were here during those turbulent years when my children swirled around my feet. Laundry, dishes, conflict, they almost overwhelmed me, but You kept me going.

I'm still in the race today and I'm still running. The obstacles are

Practicing Truth in the Family of God

different now and sometimes I have to slow down.

It seems like I have to stop more often to help a fallen sister, to straighten the path in front of a brother who's almost ready to give up.

Lord, please, keep me looking to You. And when I forget and get ugly and critical because I put too much attention on me, please, I really do want Your discipline.

It brings forth a harvest of righteousness and peace.

6

Keep on Running

Hebrews 12:14-28

❧ DAY 1 ❧

GOD SPEAKS

PEACE, HOLINESS, AND "SEEING" GOD

1. What are some things that can keep you from building an intimate relationship with someone you love?

   _____

Read **Hebrews 12:14-17**.

These verses are clear and hard-hitting. The writer of Hebrews gives his readers specifics in what they are to do, the dangers they are to avoid, and what they can learn from Old Testament history in order to run the race successfully.

Today we'll concentrate on two of these.

Practicing Truth in the Family of God

Read **Hebrews 12:14** again.

2. What image does the word *pursue* bring to your mind?

   _____

   What specifically are we to run after?

   _____

3. What happens when peace is allowed to flourish in the family?

   _____

   In the church?

   _____

4. To live at peace with others is an important command that recurs throughout Scripture. Carefully observe the following verses.

   Psalm 34:14 _____

   Romans 12:18 _____

   Romans 14:19 _____

   1 Peter 3:11 _____

   Use a concordance to help you can find others. Write down two or three of the ones that are most significant to you.

   _____

5. Holiness is set alongside peace as an object of our pursuit—we can't have one without the other. What have you already discovered about holiness in this book (Heb. 2:10-11; 10:10, 14, 29)?

   _____

Keep on Running

___

Write a brief definition of holiness. Remember, holiness is not a state of perfection, but a process of becoming more and more like Jesus.

___

6. Compare the last phrase in **Hebrews 12:14** with Jesus' words in **Matthew 5:8-9** and John's words in **1 John 3:2**. What is the result of peace and holiness in the believer's life?

___

What does it mean to you to "see God"?

___

I LISTEN

The psalmist knew that an intimate relationship with God only comes as we see God, as we look into His face (Ps. 24:3-6, 105:3-4).

Explore thoughts of peace and holiness and "seeing God" in your journal. Just as the Father invites His blind child to touch Him, to memorize His face, so God entreats us to "see Him."

WE TALK TOGETHER

Pursing peace and holiness is part of seeking His face.

Ask God to bring to your mind one person with whom He especially wants you to pursue peace. Ask Him to show you a specific action you can take to foster peace, then ask for His help as you follow through.

❦ DAY 2 ❦

GOD SPEAKS

BEWARE THE BITTER ROOT

Practicing Truth in the Family of God

Read **Hebrews 12:15-17**.
1. God often uses word pictures to communicate truth to His people. Draw a picture of what you imagine a bitter root would look like.

Yesterday we discovered two things we're to pursue—peace and holiness. Now we're given three dangers that threaten us. The NIV Bible says: "See to it that no one misses the grace of God and that no bitter root grows up to cause trouble and defile many. See that no one is sexually immoral, or is godless like Esau, who for a single meal sold his inheritance rights as the oldest son."

2. What three dangers are we to avoid?

   1. _____

   2. _____

   3. _____

The first danger we are to avoid is prefaced by the verb translated "looking diligently" and "see to it" (v. 15), and has the idea of oversight. The context is that believers must care for one another. William Barclay writes:

> There is the danger of missing the grace of God. The word he uses might be paraphrased failing to keep up with the grace of God. The early Greek commentator Theopylact interprets this in terms of a journey of a band of travellers who every now and again check up, "Has anyone fallen out? Has anyone been left behind while the others have pressed on?" In Micah there is a vivid text, "I will assemble the lame" (4:6). Moffatt translates it:

Keep on Running

"I will collect the stragglers." It is easy to straggle away, to linger behind, to drift instead of to march, and so to miss the grace of God.[1]

3. Have you known someone you think has come short of God's grace? Have you experienced it for yourself? Tell about it.

   _____

   How can we model grace in such a way that our brothers and sisters are encouraged to live in its fullness?

   _____

4. The second danger we are to avoid is _____.

Read **Deuteronomy 29:18**.
5. What additional insights do these verses give in regards to the bitter root?

   _____

   Bitterness can be against people, churches, schools, family, or employer. How can we help another when we see bitterness begining to take root?

   _____

   Bitterness, when allowed to grow, has wide-ranging effects. What are some practical steps we can take to root it out of our own lives?

   _____

The third warning reveals the danger of falling into immorality or going back into an unholy lifestyle. You may wish to read the two stories that the writer of Hebrews puts together here (Gen. 25:28-34, 27:1-40).

---

1. Barclay, p. 182.

Practicing Truth in the Family of God

Esau was a man who put his physical needs before his spiritual ones. The result was disaster—it was now impossible for him to change his mind; "he could not find a way to change what he had done."

6. What are some of the lasting consequences that come as a result of a wrong choice?

_____
_____

The question here is not one of forgiveness. God always forgives the man or woman who comes to Him. How would you counsel a young girl who has lost her virginity? A son who has lost his purity?

_____

What scripture passage could you use to bring comfort and encouragement?

_____
_____

I LISTEN

The fruitful tree described in Psalm 1 is the opposite of a bitter root bearing poisonous fruit. Draw the tree (Ps. 1) bearing the fruit of the Spirit (Gal. 5:22-23). Thinking through John 4:13-14 and Revelation 22:2 will bring added beauty.

WE TALK TOGETHER

Bitter roots keep spiritual fruit from forming in our lives. Review the fruit of the Spirit (Gal. 5:22-23). Ask God what He would have you cultivate this week.

Keep on Running

❦ DAY 3 ❦

GOD SPEAKS

THE TWO MOUNTAINS

Has anyone ever given you specific directions to a place, then said something like this: "You won't be coming this way, but right up here there's a sharp turn. If you should come too fast you could overturn. There's a cliff nearby and you could go over."

1. What would be your response to the one giving you these directions?

___

In the first chapter of Hebrews we have been given an awesome word picture of Jesus. His glory radiates from His person and we are drawn to worship.

Later we picked up a recurring theme, a whisper, an invitation: "Draw near, come into My presence. I am your High Priest, your Mediator. I want you to know Me. I want to hold you close."

We're encouraged to be women of faith. To run with endurance the race set before us.

Then suddenly a mysterious mountain rears up in front of us. Then another. What do these mountains mean?

Read Hebrews 12:18-24.

These verses contain one of the most vivid contrasts yet used by the writer. Let's look at them closely. The first mountain is one that believers today will not be coming to. The second is the one we run to.

2. Draw two mountains below. Write phrases that describe each one on each mountain (Note the word *to* in the verses in Hebrews).

You have not come to the mountain that may be touched....

Practicing Truth in the Family of God

(Exodus 19:12-13; Deut. 4:11, 5:23-27; Heb. 12:18-21).

But you have come to Mount Zion. . . .

(Heb. 12:22-24, Rev. 22:5).

3. Three things are stressed at Mount Sinai: 1) God's majesty, 2) His absolute unapproachability, 3) His terror.
   What is your emotional response to this mountain?

   _____

4. Six things await the child of God in Mount Zion, the heavenly city of God. What are they?

   1. _____
   2. _____
   3. _____
   4. _____
   5. _____
   6. _____

   Which of these details most emphasize God's grace to your own heart?

   _____

Keep on Running

What is your emotional response to this mountain?

_____

I LISTEN

Hebrews 12:24 ends with a contrast between the blood of Abel and the blood of Christ. Abel's blood cries out for vengeance; Christ's blood for reconciliation.

Choose two contrasting words or themes from this passage and do an acrostic, e.g. old and new; law and grace; darkness and light; Abel and Christ.

WE TALK TOGETHER

Tell God what it means to you to be able to enter the heavenly city and be close to Him.

🐾 DAY 4 🐾

GOD SPEAKS

A WARNING FROM HEAVEN

1. Have you ever experienced a time when you felt like your entire life was being shaken by forces outside your control? Describe your feelings.

_____

Read **Hebrews 12:18-24**.

The verses from yesterday's study remind us again of the foreboding mountain of fire and whirlwind and the "thou shalt nots." But we've run to the mountain of grace that symbolizes the presence of God. Because we've been justified by Jesus' blood we can stand confident before the Judge of all.

But wait. A voice blasts our ears. Our hearts tremble. It is a warning from our Coach.

Read **Hebrews 12:25-28**.

Practicing Truth in the Family of God

2. Prayerfully read and reread, then write down as many observations as you can about the passage. Pay particular attention to contrasts and pronouns. (Three groups of people are addressed here. We're one of them!)

_____

_____

_____

Compare **Hebrews 12:25** with **Hebrews 2:2-3**.

3. What are we being warned not to do?

_____

4. The phrase, "yet once more," in **Hebrews 12:26-27** is repeated twice and is from **Haggai 2:6**. Condense your thoughts on these verses into one or two sentences for each question.

    What is the author saying?

    _____

    What is he saying about it?

    _____

The earth shook when Jesus died and when He arose (Matt. 27:51, 28:2). Both heaven and earth will shake when He comes again (Heb. 12:27).

5. What more do you discover about His second coming in these verses?

    Matthew 24:29 _____

    2 Peter 3:10 _____

Keep on Running

6. Isaiah also saw the end of this present world. What more do you discover about the end as he saw it?

Isaiah 66:17, 22 _____

I LISTEN

Complete this sentence: Because God is going to do what He says He will do, I need to . . . .

Continue to write as His Holy Spirit speaks to your heart.

WE TALK TOGETHER

Ask God to help you listen, really listen, to what He said to you in His Word today.

🍇 DAY 5 🍇

GOD SPEAKS

How Shall We Come into His Presence?

A teacher of teens asked her students what they thought the phrase, "The fear of the Lord" meant.

One boy said, "I think it's being sort of scared. Not like God's your best friend at all. Instead He's far away—up there in the sky. When you do something wrong, your stomach knots up tight."

A girl said, "The fear of the Lord means reverence. Thinking about how great God is makes me want to be still. I think it's why I talk soft when I pray out loud."

1. What about you? What would you say?

_____

Read **Hebrews 12:28-29**.

These last two verses flow from those which precede it and form a beautiful conclusion. Read it in several translations. For example the NASB says: "Therefore, since we receive a kingdom which cannot be

Practicing Truth in the Family of God

shaken, let us show gratitude, by which we may offer to God an acceptable service with reverence and awe. For our God is a consuming fire."

2. What are some of the ways the phrases, "let us have grace," "serve God," and "godly fear" have been translated in other translations?

   _____

   Which translation of each phrase is most meaningful to you? Why?

   _____

   _____

   The phrase *godly fear* is closely related to the Old Testament phrase *the fear of the Lord*. The NIV Study Bible describes the "fear of the Lord" as "loving reverence for God that includes submission to his lordship and the commands of his word."
   The words *honor, revere,* and *reverence* can help us further understand the fear of the Lord. *Respect* is a common denominator in each of these. Look them up in a dictionary.

3. Write down phrases that help you better understand the biblical meaning of these words:

   Honor _____

   Revere _____

   Reverence _____

4. Look up the word *fear* in a concordance. Select several references that pertain to "the fear of the Lord" and look them up. What more did you discover about "godly fear"?

   _____

Keep on Running

What does it mean to you to serve God acceptably with reverence and godly fear?

_____

The last verse (Heb. 12:28) brings us back to Mt. Sinai. Yes, the arrangement is different now—we have a new mountain, a new covenant. But God hasn't changed. He's still a consuming fire.

5. Why do you think the writer chose this particular word picture of God to conclude this section on the race?

_____

Challenge activity: Hebrews 12 is a chapter on running the race. Review key concepts for successfully finishing the race by completing the following sentences:

In verse 1 we're told to run with _____.

In verses 2 and 3 we're told to fix our eyes on _____,

lest we become _____. In verses 4-11

we're reminded that God's discipline _____.

Verses 12-14 give us four commands for successfully running. We're

to lift up _____, we're to help _____

by _____, we're to pursue _____

and _____. In verses 15-17 we're warned about

the _____ that can contaminate many.

Verses 18-24 both warn and encourage us. We aren't running to a

mountain of fear but to a mountain characterized by _____.

Practicing Truth in the Family of God

According to verses 25-29 we are receiving _____.

Therefore we are called to serve God with _____

and _____ fear. For our God is a _____.

I LISTEN

We are created to sing and shout aloud to our Lord, to offer Him our thanksgiving and extol him with music. When we do we acknowledge His greatness, His holiness, His authority as King. But there's more. Our God is a consuming fire.

Fire cleanses.

Prayerfully read Isaiah 6:1-7. Write a personal response to the Holy God whose glory fills the earth.

I WORSHIP HIM

Worship Him as the God of fire.

WALKING ALONG TOGETHER

The red hot coals beneath the blackened cast iron grill whisper softly. Close to the grill's edge, tiny pancake batter spills form miniature circles smaller than buttons. I catch them with my turner and flick them into the fire.

"Why do you do that, Grandma?" my six-year-old grandson asks.

"For the fire fairies," I say.

We peer into the fire together—the coals shimmer gold—red—orange.

Our God Is a Consuming Fire

Another fire, another coal—red hot from the heart of the altar in the temple.

I shiver. Isaiah—what must it have been like for him to have a live coal touch his lips? A heavenly vision. Isaiah sees the Lord sitting on this throne. His glory fills the temple.

> And the posts of the door were shaken by the voice of him who cried out, and the house was filled with smoke.
> Then I said: "Woe is me, for I am undone! Because I am a

man of unclean lips, and I dwell in the midst of a people of unclean lips; for my eyes have seen the King, The LORD of hosts."

Then one of the seraphim flew to me, having in his hand a live coal which he had taken with the tongs from the altar.

And he touched my mouth with it, and said: "Behold, this has touched your lips; your iniquity is taken away, and your sin purged" (Isa. 6:4-7).

The God who called to Isaiah from His throne is a holy God. He is a King and Kings have kingdoms.

Since I'm receiving a kingdom which can't be shaken, He's asking me to serve Him with reverence and holy fear. He's asking me to come into His presence. He wants to remove those things from my life that would keep me at a distance. Those things that would keep me from successfully running the race set before me.

He's reminding me again that He is a consuming fire.

Burning Up the Garbage

As a child, nothing fascinated me quite like fire. A used sheet torn from a writing tablet, an empty shredded wheat box illustrated with a foaming Niagara Falls, a blue salt box with Miss Morton under her umbrella, eternally pouring....

I'd shove them into the kitchen stove and hold the lid open as long as I dared. There was something so satisfying about watching the paper that so quickly turned to clutter in the house, catch fire and disappear.

Later, as a young mother with children of my own, I'd take the week's burnable garbage outside to our burn pile. While the little ones napped, I'd strike a match and remember Hebrews 12:29, "for our God is a consuming fire." An unearthly joy would course through me as tiny tongues of flame licked at the brown paper bags and the empty cornflake boxes.

The hour I burned the garbage became a time of worship as I brought before my Lord the sins that so easily entangled—a cutting tongue, an impatient spirit. I brought the things that encumbered me—the house that wouldn't stay clean no matter how hard I tried, the leaks that appeared whenever it rained.

It wasn't just my garbage that disappeared into ashes. God had

Practicing Truth in the Family of God

taken His holy coal and cleansed my heart. I had looked into His face, been strengthened and renewed. I was ready to return to my family, ready to continue on....

My God Is a Consuming Fire

My grandson is asleep in his tent now. I return to mine, rummage for a flashlight, Bible, and journal.

The fire glows. The flashlight circles God's Words in light: "Therefore, since we are receiving a kingdom which cannot be shaken, let us have grace, by which we may serve God acceptably with reverence and godly fear; for our God is a consuming fire" (Heb. 12:28-29).

I continue reading. "Let brotherly love continue" (Heb. 13:1), then write: *But love has to flow from the altar of sacrifice, doesn't it, Lord? If I'm to love my brothers and sisters the way you want me to love them, then I must be cleansed.*

I tear a sheet from my notebook: *resentment toward Derek, desire for people approval, fear of the future....*

After awhile I crumble the sheet into a wad and place it in the campfire. The coals fan into tiny tongues of flame. The paper crumbles into ashes.

My God is a consuming fire. By His grace I can continue.

7

Let Love Continue...
Hebrews 13:1-10

❧ DAY 1 ❧

GOD SPEAKS

BROTHERS, STRANGERS, AND PRISONERS

1. What is your definition of entertainment?

   _____

   Of hospitality?

   _____

Some commentators think the exhortations in this chapter are unrelated. Charles Swindoll writes: "There is no logical flow to chapter 13." It is "... comprised of snippets of last-minute instructions

Practicing Truth in the Family of God

and practical advice."[1]

Simon Kistemaker, however, sees chapter 13 as "the hand of a literary artist at work in the construction of this passage."[2] You'll want to keep both views in mind as you study.

Read **Hebrews 13:1-3**.

2. The Greek word for "love" as used here is *philadelphia* which means brotherly love. It carries with it a sense of family warmth and affection. Look up these scriptures: Romans 12:9-10, 1 Thessalonians 4:9-10, 1 Peter 1:22, and write a description of this kind of love.

   _____

   _____

Brotherly love begins with the family, then spreads outward. The reader is next encouraged to entertain strangers. The NASB gives additional insight: "Do not neglect to show hospitality to strangers, for by this some have entertained angels without knowing it."

3. What is the writer reminding his readers of in this verse?

   _____

   Is "practicing hospitality" the same as "entertaining friends and aquaintances"? Why or why not?

   _____

   Why is it often so easy to "forget" or "neglect" to practice hospitality to those outside the family of God?

   _____

---

1. Swindoll, p. 86.
2. Simon J. Kistemaker, *New Testment Commentary: Hebrews* (Grand Rapids, MI: Baker Book House Company, 1986), p. 407.

Let Love Continue . . .

There is a third responsibility found in Hebrews 13:1-3. What is it?

_____

At the time this letter was written, many believers had been imprisoned because of their faith. Earlier the readers had been commended for their care of prisoners (Heb. 10:34). Now the writer reminds them, "Remember those in prison as if you were their fellow prisoners, and those who are mistreated as if you yourselves were suffering" (NIV).

What does this verse suggest about empathy?

_____

In ancient times, prisoners were dependent on family and friends to provide for their physical needs. If the family didn't, the prisoner suffered. How can we apply this concept of meeting physical needs, particularly in the family of God?

_____

5. Prisons today are different than they once were. Yet all around us are men and women who are in their own personal cells—a loveless marriage, a dead-end job, a restricting handicap. Describe how you could go about meeting one of these needs.

_____

Compare **Matthew 25:32-40** to **Hebrews 13:2-3**.
6. What additional insights do Jesus' words give about meeting the needs of strangers and prisoners?

_____

Read **Hebrews 13:1-3** again.
7. How do the exhortations to help the stranger, the prisoners, and

Practicing Truth in the Family of God

those who are suffering fulfill Christ's command to "love your neighbor as yourself"?

_____

I LISTEN

Today's scripture contains three statements that address three areas of need—"Love your brothers, entertain strangers, remember the prisoners." Choose one of these statements and explain how you could begin to make it a part of your lifestyle.

WE TALK TOGETHER

Talk to God about what you wrote in your journal. Ask Him to show you additional details on how you can put it into action.

❦ DAY 2 ❦

GOD SPEAKS

MARRIAGE

1. What does marriage mean to you? On a scale of 1 to 10, how would you evaluate your commitment to marriage and sexual purity?

   _____

Read **Hebrews 13:4** in the NIV.
2. What are the two commands given in this verse?

   _____

   What is the warning?

   _____

3. Define these key words:

Let Love Continue . . .

honorable _____

undefiled _____

fornicators _____

adulterers _____

judge _____

4. The Greek word for *undefiled* means "free from contamination." How can men and women defile the marriage bed?

   _____

   What does God say He will do to those who choose sexual impurity?

   _____

Read **1 Corinthians 6:18-20**.
5. Adultery and fornication not only destroy marriages and bring us under God's judgment, they also have power to destroy the heart of who we are. What are some practical things we can do to avoid falling into this sin that is so prevalent today?

   _____

I LISTEN

God's judgment on sexual sins always results in a loss of vitality. Psalm 32 is a description of what David went through after he committed adultery with Bethsheba. As you read it, pay particular attention to verses 3 and 4. Describe what is happening in David's heart in each phrase.

Paraphrase Psalm 32:5 and Psalm 51:12-13 into your own words. How could you use these verses to bring hope to someone caught in sexual impurity?

WE TALK TOGETHER

Practicing Truth in the Family of God

Obedience to God's commands concerning sexual morality means we escape God's judgment. But there's more. If you're married, ask God to show you ways you can cultivate your marriage. If you're unmarried, ask Him to help you honor the marriage vows of others and make a commitment to sexual purity.

❧ DAY 3 ❧

GOD SPEAKS

CONDUCT, COVETOUSNESS, AND CONTENTMENT

1. What kind of problems have you experienced at home or church as a result of wanting something that belonged to another person?

   _____

Read **Hebrews 13:5-6**.
2. List the commands in verse 5.

   1. _____

   2. _____

   Define the key words:

   Conduct _____

   Coveteousness _____

   Content _____

   Circle the word *for* in the middle of the verse. Complete this sentence: Instead of wanting someone's else money, husband, or possessions, I can be content because _____

   _____.

112

Let Love Continue . . .

Verse 6 reminds us again of how the writer of Hebrews feels about the Old Testament scriptures. He knows that God is the author and when God speaks, he had better listen.

The exact location of the quotation introduced with the words, *"For He, Himself has said,"* is uncertain. However the basic concept it teaches appears in various forms in various places.

3. Write down God's assurances to His people from the following verses:

   Genesis 28:15: _____

   Deut. 31:6,8: _____

   Joshua 1:5: _____

   1 Chr. 28:20: _____

   Put a star alongside the one that is most helpful for you right now.

Compare **Hebrews 13:6** with **Psalm 118:5-6**.

4. Who answered the psalmist in Psalm 118:5?

   _____

   Who is speaking in Psalm 118:6?

   _____

   In Hebrews 13:6?

   _____

   Paraphrase Psalm 118:6 into your own words. "It is better to take refuge in the Lord than to trust in my monthly paycheck. . . ."

   _____

5. How does putting our trust in God rather than in things guard us against coventousness?

Practicing Truth in the Family of God

_____

How does it cultivate contentment?

_____

I LISTEN

A young woman in deep distress over her marriage sat in a park with her arms clasped around her knees, pouring her pain out to God. Afterwards she sat very still. Had God heard her prayer? Would He help her?

A glint of copper in a dirt-clod—she reached out her hand. As the dirt fell away, she read God's message written on the penny—*in God we trust.*

Today that woman carries an oversized penny on a key ring wherever she goes. It is her testimony of her faith in God.

Draw a penny in your journal. Underneath write, *Lord, teach me to trust.*

WE TALK TOGETHER

"Casting all your care upon Him, for He cares for you (1 Pet.5:7).

🐛 DAY 4 🐛

GOD SPEAKS

REMEMBER GODLY LEADERS

1. Think back over your life. Who were the people who stand out in your memory? Write down the names of three people who taught you principles from God's Word by word and example.

_____

Let Love Continue . . .

Read **Hebrews 13:7-8**.

The writer of Hebrews has some advice to give his readers regarding their relationships with those who ruled over them as their spiritual leaders. (The NASB describes them as, "those who led us." The NIV says, "Remember your leaders, who spoke the word of God to you. Consider the outcome of their way of life and imitate their faith.")

2. What two commands are given in verse 7?

    1. _____

    2. _____

3. The verb *remember* means to "call back to mind what you know about a person"; consider to "observe carefully, investigate." How does following this bit of advice protect you from the destruction that comes from following an ungodly leader?

    _____

4. Look back at the names you wrote down in question 1. Choose one to concentrate on right now. What do you remember most about that person?

    _____

    What comes to your mind as you carefully observe the way he lived his life?

    _____

    What specifics do you recall? For example, what stories did your parents tell you that made you want to follow Jesus? How did that pastor encourage you to keep on perservering? What special tips for ministry did you learn from the youth leader who always had time to listen?

    _____

Practicing Truth in the Family of God

How can you imitate it?

_____

5. Three times in this chapter the writer stresses those who "rule over us." What does he ask his readers to do in each instance.

   v. 7: _____

   v. 17: _____

   v. 24: _____

6. What is to be our attitude regarding godly leaders?

   _____

   What happens to our leaders when we resist them (v. 17)?

   _____

7. That Jesus is the ultimate leader is alluded to in verse 8. As we examine His life from beginning to end, what do we see?

   _____

I LISTEN

Evaluate your responsibilities and attitudes toward the spiritual leaders God has placed in your home and church or place of ministry. How can you make their ministry a joy?

WE TALK TOGETHER

Ask God to guard you and those you love against ungodly leadership. Pray for discernment. Remember each of your leaders to Jesus Christ who is the same yesterday, today, and forever.

Let Love Continue . . .

🐞 DAY 5 🐞

GOD SPEAKS

WATCH OUT FOR FALSE TEACHING

1. Although churches that preach and teach God's Word are growing, so are the cults and sects. Why do you think this is so?

   _____

Yesterday we caught a glimpse of our unchanging Lord Jesus Christ. Today we'll look at the grace that has the power to keep us from being carried away by false teachings.

Read **Hebrews 13:9-10**.
   Charles Swindoll points out that the word *varied* (various) in v. 9 is from the Greek word from which we get the word *polka dot*. He pictures for us a variety of colors that pleases the eyes and the senses. Red dots to stimulate our passions, cool blue ones to appeal to our intellect. And what about the gold ones that promise fame and money, gray ones that tempt us to compromise the truth of God's Word? [3]

2. What is the result when people feed on these strange doctrines rather than the grace of God?

   _____

   Complete this sentence: The grace of God _____

   whereas foods are _____

Read **Hebrews 13:10**.
This verse emphasizes the spiritual even more than verse 9 does. In chapters 9 and 10 the writer has repeatedly taught that Christ offered

---

3. Swindoll, p. 114

Practicing Truth in the Family of God

Himself once for all (Heb. 9:25-26, 28; 10:10, 12, 14). We can know that the phrase, "we have an altar" symbolizes the cross.

3. The contrast between the false teaching in v. 9 and the cross in v. 10 is vivid, almost startling. Sketch a picture of a cross overshadowing a banner with various colored polka dots representing various false doctrines. Create a title for your drawing.

The Old Testament priests didn't have the right to eat from the altar, but we do. Those who come to Jesus by faith have access to the presence of God. But there's more. Jesus Himself invites us to participate fully in His life and death.

Read **John 6:53.**
4. What does He tell us to do?

___

Read **John 6:58.**
5. What does He promise?

___

Hebrews 13:10 is a vivid reminder that Christ's sacrificial work is far greater than the animal sacrifices of the Old Testament. Once again the writer is emphasizing the major theme of this epistle. Jesus Christ is a superior High Priest.

The verses that follow develop more fully the theme of Christ's sacrifice. We'll explore them next week.

Let Love Continue . . .

Challenge Activity: Choose an older person who possesses a quality of faith you would like to imitate and interview him or her. Who led him to Jesus? What scriptures have most impacted his life? Ask him what events in his life increased his faith. Record your findings in your journal and consider how you might follow them.

I LISTEN

The cross reminds us of the magnitude of Christ's sacrifice. If possible, find the hymn, "The Old Rugged Cross." Either write the words in your journal as an expression of your worship or write your own song extolling the cross and what it represents to you.

I WORSHIP HIM

Sing to the Lord the song you wrote in your journal.

WALKING ALONG TOGETHER

Last night I sat on the couch surrounded by books. "Have you solved all the problems of the world?" my husband Bud asked as he sat down on a chair opposite me.

"No. But I've made a good start. Listen to this: 'Let love continue,' 'Show hospitality,' 'Remember the prisoners,' 'Let marriage be held in honor.' And then the writer talks about money and contentment and leadership."

I leaned forward. "I'm on the thirteenth chapter, Bud. Up to now Hebrews has been mostly about a Christian's relationship to God. This last chapter focuses on the relationship of one with another."

"Like practical maybe?"

I nodded. "A good way to end a book, too. Most women like that practical touch. Home. The children in bed. A warm fire." After Bud went to bed I looked at the observations I'd written in my notebook. "I don't see any logical flow here," I muttered. "I keep feeling like I'm missing something."

If I were, it wouldn't be the first time I'd missed something important and come up with a wrong conclusion. Like the time I misinterpreted truth and did acts of brotherly love and kindness with the wrong motive.

A Verse out of Context

I was probably eight or nine at the time, and I was mad at my

Practicing Truth in the Family of God

brother, Lawrence. Dale and I always had to obey the rules but Lawrence and his smooth silver tongue could talk Mother into letting him do anything—have anything.

It wasn't fair.

I decided to get even. My job was to make all the beds in the house. Instead of pulling Lawrence's sheets smooth, I left the lumps and carefully smoothed the blanket over the top so no one would know.

When Lawrence wanted to talk to me, I'd clamp my mouth shut and refuse to answer. Other times I'd disagree with everything he said. It wasn't long before we were squabbling something fierce.

My mother took me aside. "Eva Jane," she said. "The Bible says we're to love our brothers."

"He's mean," I said. "He's always picking on me."

She tried again. "Jesus said that we're to love those who despitefully use us."

I wasn't impressed.

She continued. "He said that when we're kind to those who hurt us, it's like heaping coals of fire on their heads."

A picture leaped into my mind. It was a wonderful picture.

"I wonder why He said that," Mother said almost as an afterthought.

Excitement coursed through me. I didn't wonder why God said it—I knew why. It was for me.

Heaping Coals on Lawrence's Head

The next morning I smoothed the lumps out of Lawrence's bed. I smiled as I did it. I was heaping burning hot coals on top of his poor defenseless head.

That day I listened to his stories. I smiled and nodded and we talked and talked. At suppertime I put the prettiest plate at his place and lined up the fork, spoon, and knife just so. Over Lawrence's head, God stood poised, a great shovelful of smoking coals in His hand.

My mother was elated with my progress. She put her arm around me and whispered, "You're growing into such a lovely young lady."

I have no idea how long my coal dumping stage lasted. I do know now that my thinking was all wrong. I had misinterpreted God and His Word and used it for my own selfish purposes.

Even though I smile as I recall my childish thoughts and actions, there's a warning for me too. I don't want to ever take God's Word

Let Love Continue . . .

lightly as I seek to write and teach others. I long to be a careful student of His book.

I reach for my pen. Maybe those who say this chapter is left over bits and pieces of instructions are right. Lord, help me understand.

It is as I'm in the actual process of writing a chapter summary that understanding begins to flash.

Beginning to Summarize

Chapter 13 opens with the exhortation to let brotherly love continue in the family of God. From that love should flow a love for others. We're commanded to show hospitality to strangers, to have empathy for prisoners and meet their needs.

Both brotherly love and love for those outside of Christ are best expressed in a love within the context of the family. Therefore the warning: marital love is to be untainted by adultery and coveteousness. Our love is also expressed in contentment and by respect for the leaders who proclaim the Word and teach the gospel. We're not to depart from that Word but rather allow it to minister God's grace to us.

The writer calls the readers back to the heart of Hebrews with his use of the word, altar.

I put down my pencil. He's reminding me again to focus on Jesus. When I do, I'll overflow with right attitudes and right actions.

Although I'm not yet ready to finish my summary, I'm beginning to see a flow of thought. It is a crimson cord that connects the verses and makes the chapter a literary masterpiece of art.

I reach for a red pen. I'll look more closely at the section on the cross tomorrow.

Tonight I sketch a cross in my Bible. The top begins at the altar in verse 10 and continues down through verse 16.

Before I go to bed, I bow my head. *Lord, don't ever let me forget that your sacrifice for my sins and the sins of the whole world is the very heart of the book of Hebrews.*

Let love continue on in my family, in the family of God. Make it the crimson cord that binds our hearts together.

8

Grace Be with You All . . .

Hebrews 13:11-25

❧ DAY 1 ❧

GOD SPEAKS

OUR HIGH HOLY PRIEST

1. Which bit of practical advice from the first part of chapter 13 did you put into practice last week? Tell about it.

   _____

   Chapter 13 begins with a series of exhortations. Running the race successfully means we're going to have to pay attention to details.
   A subtle change occurs in verse 10—the writer is drawing us back to the heart of Christ's sacrifice. Words like *altar, blood, high priest,* and *sanctify* help us remember.

Practicing Truth in the Family of God

Read Hebrews 13:10-14.

2. Write down additional words that point to Jesus' sacrifice for sins.

   _____

3. Read these verses in several translations if you have access to them. What further insights do you discover?

   _____

Earlier in Hebrews we saw that the Day of Atonement foreshadowed the atoning work of Jesus. On that day the high priest brought the blood of the sacrificial animals into the Most Holy Place (Lev. 16:14-15) but the bodies were burned outside the camp (Lev. 16:27).

Read John 19:17-18.

4. Jesus' death outside the gates of Jerusalem symbolized His rejection by the Jewish leaders. According to Hebrews 13:12, what was His purpose in His reproach and suffering?

   _____

5. Earlier verses in Hebrews revealed more about Jesus' making His people holy through His blood. Look up the following verses. Find phrases that talk about holiness and sanctification.

   Hebrews 2:11 _____

   Hebrews 10:10, 14 _____

   Hebrews 12:14 _____

Read **Hebrews 13:13-14** again.

6. Verse 13 contains an appeal. What is it?

   _____

Grace Be with You All . . .

How does Moses' life encourage you to accept reproach for Christ's sake (Heb. 11:26)?

_____

Have you ever experienced reproach as a result of identifying with Christ? How did you handle it?

_____

How would you encourage a new believer who was being rejected by unbelieving peers?

_____

7. What important truth are you reminded of in verse 14?

_____

How does Abraham encourage you to seek a heavenly city rather than an earthly one (Heb. 11:9, 10, 13-16)?

_____

How does seeking a heavenly city affect the way you spend your money?

_____

Your time?

_____

I LISTEN

Amy Carmichael wrote that there is always something more in your nature that God wants to mark with the cross. Put this phrase alongside Hebrews 13:10-15. What more in your nature might God want to mark with His cross?

Practicing Truth in the Family of God

WE TALK TOGETHER

Ask Him to draw you into a willingness to "go forth to Him outside the gate."

❦ DAY 2 ❦

GOD SPEAKS

SACRIFICES WE CAN BRING

1. Have you ever experienced a time when praising God was the last thing you wanted to do? Tell about it.

   _____

   Read **Hebrews 13:15-17**.
2. Circle the word *therefore*, then look at the preceding verses. Identify at least two things for which you can praise God.

   _____

   _____

3. The word *sacrifice* is an important word in these verses. Look it up in the dictionary, compare it with what you've already learned about sacrifice in Hebrews, then write a definition.

   _____

4. We know from the preceding verses that we no longer have an altar where animal sacrifices are brought. But that doesn't mean that we aren't to offer God spiritual sacrifices. What more do you learn about the sacrifice of praise from the following verses?

   Leviticus 7:12-15 _____

   Psalm 107:21-22 _____

Grace Be with You All . . .

Isaiah 57:19 _____

Hosea 14:2 _____

Ephesians 5:20 _____

1 Thessalonians 5:18 _____

5. Another kind of spiritual sacrifice is spoken of in verse 16. What is it?

   _____

   The Amplified Bible puts it even more clearly:

   Do not forget or neglect to do kindness and good, to be generous and distribute and contribute to the needy {of the church as embodiment and proof of fellowship}, for such sacrifices are well-pleasing to God.

   What is God's attitude toward these sacrifices?

   _____

6. To "do good" is a general term, but "to share" is specific. We are to share what we have: money, possessions, our time, our love. The following scriptures help us to be even more specific.

   Exodus 35:4-19 _____

   Romans 12:1-2 _____

   Philippians 4:10, 18 _____

7. Earlier we looked at Hebrews 13:17 in the context of Hebrews 13:7. Let's come at it now from a different perspective. Have you ever thought of your submisssion to those in spiritual authority over you as a sacrifice to your Lord? How might this concept take

Practicing Truth in the Family of God

away the hard part of submission and bring glory to God?

_____

I LISTEN

God wants us to praise Him with our lips, our hands, and our attitudes. Simon J. Kistemaker in his *New Testament Commentary: Hebrews* says:

> In a word game, arranging the letters *g o o d* is relatively simple. The same set of letters, however, can also be divided into two words that read, "Go do!" That means translating the word into deed. I must go and do to be good in the sight of God.[1]

Draw an arrow in your journal. Above it write "Go do!" Give the Holy Spirit the opportunity to show you a specific "go do" He wants you to do today.

I WORSHIP HIM

Hebrews 13:5 and 8 contain two significant truths about Jesus. Use these truths in a praise song directed to Him.

❦ DAY 3 ❦

GOD SPEAKS

PRAY FOR US

1. Someone has said, "The greatest thing you can do for someone is to pray for them." Do you agree or disagree with this statement?

   _____

2. Using a dictionary, define both pray and praise.

   _____

_____

1. Kistemaker, p. 424.

Grace Be with You All . . .

How do they differ?

_____

Read **Hebrews 13:18-19**.
3. What does the writer's entreaty, "pray for us," tell you about his attitude toward God?

_____

His attitude toward those he writes to?

_____

4. The word *desiring* conveys the idea of being "bound and determined"? According to verse 18 what is the writer determined to do?

_____

Compare your own heart desire to that of the writer. How do you measure up?

_____

In verse 19, the writer gives a specific prayer request. He longed to be with them, to see them face to face. It was the desire of his heart.

5. What is the desire of your heart? Write it down in one or two sentences, then pray about sharing it with a trusted friend.

_____

6. The writer to the Hebrews isn't the only New Testament writer who requests prayer for himself. Paul often asked his readers to pray for him. According to the following verses, what are some of his requests?

Romans 15:30-32_____

Practicing Truth in the Family of God

    2 Corinthians 1:11-12 _____

    Colossians 4:3-4 _____

    2 Thessalonians 3:1 _____

Read Ephesians 6:18-20.

Paul is not only instructing the Ephesian Christians to pray for him and his ministry, he's telling them to pray for all the saints. But how do we do it?

7. The following questions are designed to help you think through practical ways that will help you pray more effectively for others. Begin by listing the people who need your prayers.

    _____

    _____

    How can you pray for all of these within your available time?

    _____

    How can you remind yourself to pray for them?

    _____

    What would you pray for each?

    _____

    How will you know when God has answered a particular request?[2]

    _____

---

2. Eileen Pollinger, *Building Christian Discipline* (Minneapolis, MN: Bethany House, 1986), p. 13.

Grace Be with You All . . .

I LISTEN

Ask a friend to share a prayer request about which you can pray. Write it in your journal and tell your friend you are making a commitment to pray for the request each day this week. Check back in a week or so for an update.

WE TALK TOGETHER

The disciples said to Jesus, "Lord, teach us to pray." This is something you can verbalize to Him. Do it today.

❦ DAY 4 ❦

GOD SPEAKS

THE GREAT SHEPHERD

Read **Hebrews 13:20-21.**
1. Imagine that you are in church service. The pastor has read the words of the letter to the Hebrews. Now you hear the words of this benediction for the first time.

   What do you hear in the depths of your soul?

   _____

   What do you see with your spiritual eyes?

   _____

   What do you feel?

   _____

In the preceding verses (vv. 18-19) the writer had requested prayer for himself. Now he is praying for his readers—men and women who are being persecuted, who are ready to lose heart, who are in danger of turning away from Christ. It is a beautiful prayer.

Practicing Truth in the Family of God

2. Write down the names and phrases that describe Jesus in verse 20. Include one or two cross-references with each one.

   _____

3. This benediction (vv. 20-21) gathers up several themes that have meant much to the writer—peace, blood, the eternal covenant, becoming complete in Him. It also introduces two truths he has not dealt with but which are taught elsewhere in scripture. What are they?

   1. (John 10:11) _____

   2. (Romans 1:4) _____

4. This is the first time that the writer has called Jesus, the great Shepherd. How has Jesus revealed Himself to you as the great Shepherd?

   _____

Simon J. Kistemaker writes:

The metaphor of the shepherd who dies for his sheep is equivalent to that of the high priest who offers himself as a sacrifice for his people. Especially the adjective *great* is telling, for the writer of Hebrews calls Jesus the great High Priest (4:14). The two concepts, then, complement each other, although as Guthrie observes, "There is a tender aspect to the shepherd figure which is not as vivid in the high priest."[3]

5. The second part of the benediction reveals two things the great Shepherd of the sheep is doing in His people. What are they?

   1. _____

   2. _____

---

3. Kistemaker, p. 430.

Grace Be with You All . . .

Several translations use the word *equip* for the words, "make you complete." This word carries the idea of "restoring, helping along, giving encouraging thoughts." Leon Morris explains the term as used in the context of Hebrews.

> The verb "equip" (Katarizo) is often used of mending what is broken and torn, and some see a reference to putting right what was amiss in the spiritual life of the readers. A prayer that God would put things right would be quite in place. But in this context perhaps the meaning is "supply you with what you need to live the Christian life. "[4]

The Apostle Peter ties into a similar thought with these words from 2 Peter 1:3:

> "His divine power has given us everything we need for life and godliness; through our knowledge of him who called us by his own glory and goodness" (NIV).

6. How does it make you feel to realize that God accepts the ultimate responsibility of working in you "what is pleasing in His sight, through Jesus Christ"?

_____

7. Who then deserves the glory for anything good that comes from our lives?

_____

I LISTEN

The verses in our study today convey the same beauty and majesty with which the writer begins the book of Hebrews. Write the phrases in Hebrews 1:2-3 that describe Jesus in your journal. Include the names and phrases from Hebrews 13:20 from question 2.

_____

4. *The Expositor's Bible Commentary,* gen. ed. Frank E. Gaebelein (Grand Rapids, MI: Zondervan Publishing House, Regency Reference Library, 1982), vol. 12, p. 155.

Practicing Truth in the Family of God

WE TALK TOGETHER

The writer's desire for the believers was that they be fully fitted for their tasks. Ask God to make up in you that which you lack. He wants to make you complete in Jesus Christ.

❦ DAY 5 ❦

GOD SPEAKS

A GRACEFUL POSTSCRIPT

1. Do you ever add a P.S. at the end of a letter you've written? What were some of the things you added? A newsworthy item? Something you forgot to say earlier? Something you wanted to emphasize?

   _____

   _____

Read **Hebrews 13:22-25**.

2. These verses are a postscript. In it the writer turns his attention to God's people. They are also his people. What affectionate title does he use to address them?

   _____

   What is he urging them to do?

   _____

   _____

3. The process of *bearing with* means to listen, to endure, to stay with it. But listening is only the beginning. There must be personal and practical applications to this letter he designates as a

   _____

Grace Be with You All . . .

Do you wonder why the writer described his letter as being a short letter? Charles R. Erdman has this to say:

> "If Christ is the only Saviour, if he is the complete and final Revelation of God to man, if through him real and immediate access to God is possible, then an exhortation to those in peril of turning away from Christ might seem to the writer all too brief."[5]

Following the entreaty to bear with his words, he instructs us to notice the people of God. He does this by first mentioning Timothy, his recent release, and his soon coming to them.

4. What a reminder to us to reach out to the family of God. Who are some brothers or sisters you need to notice right now?

   _____

   How might you be able to minister to them?

   _____

   _____

5. His next instructions were to greet and receive greetings. This reveals the affectionate warmth of the believers in the early church. On a scale of 1-10 how would you rate your involvement with other believers.

Reread the **last three chapters of Hebrews.**
6. What lesson in faith has most strengthened your trust in God?

   _____

   _____

---

5. Charles R. Erdman, *The Epistle to the Hebrews* (Philadelphia, PA: The Westminster Press, 1934), p. 137.

Practicing Truth in the Family of God

What practical application from these chapters has made the most significant difference in your relationship with others these past eight weeks?

_____

7. The last verse in the letter is a final benediction, a prayer that God's blessing may rest on all who read this letter. How does it make you feel to realize that you are part of that *all*?

_____

Challenge Activity: You've studied in depth the letter to the Hebrews. You've done word studies and looked up cross references. You've allowed the Holy Spirit to show you practical ways to apply truth. Now the ideal thing is to read it through in a single sitting.

Remember, it's a letter. Ignore chapter and verse divisions. Simply read. You will be blessed to discover how much you understand.

You are now more fully equipped to practice truth in the family of God.

I LISTEN
Write a letter to a friend who is going through a hard time. You might want to include an encouraging verse as a postscript, e.g. Hebrews 13:5; Isaiah 40:11, 31.

WE TALK TOGETHER
Grace is God doing for a person what he or she can't do for herself. Ask God to empower your letter with His grace.

WALKING ALONG TOGETHER
I cleaned out my Hebrew files today. As I went through the last one I discovered an analogy I'd written. In it I had compared a traveler coming in on an airplane to a student of God's Word.

That student would observe the big picture as she read through a book. Then she would analyze and think through each chapter and its various parts. Sometimes word studies and topic studies would be part of it.

Grace Be with You All . . .

The traveler first observed the patchwork beauty of the countryside from the airplane—gold fields of grain, patches of green trees; a river winding through it—a distant mountain, or was it two?

As soon as she was on the ground, she began to explore what she'd only glimpsed from the air. She scrutinized a leaf skeleton submerged in a stream, noted the various bark on the trunks of trees. The king's palace overlooking the village had been the first place she'd gone. She'd been allowed into the throne room of a King. She'd seen angels. . . .

After she left the palace she'd walked down the hill. A winding road led through whispering willows and silent firs, down into a valley.

A warning sign flashed alongside a sharp curve. "Pay close attention." Another flash, "Don't drift." She stopped to examine the warning sign—to analyze its contents for herself—for other travelers who would be coming along but who might miss it.

After she deciphered the meaning of the warning, she continued on. The valley was shadowed but a song wafted up from below—a joyous song of praise and victory.

She stepped around the curve, almost missed the road sign half hidden by a sprawling grape vine. There was a cross engraved on the wood. The arrow beside it pointed down into the valley.

Later on she observed other warning flares placed alongside the road. She had even entered a sanctuary of worship, had trembled as she experienced the glory of the holy of holies. Later she'd pondered over the headstones in a cemetery reserved for heroes of faith.

And that wasn't all. She'd been a participant in a race in a sports arena, heard the spectators wildly cheer her on.

She had explored the two mountains she'd seen at a distance. One had spewed out smoke and fire, the other had invited with lush green and the sound of music. She'd even been a guest in a home where marriage was honored and people lived out their faith in practical ways.

Yes, my study of the letter to the Hebrews has been a lot like that traveler's experience as she explored new territory.

Except . . . except. . . .

Practicing Truth in the Family of God

A Backwards Look

"Lord, I'm tired. I've been knocked down more times than I care to admit since I first started writing this series. Once I just sat there for awhile. I didn't want to ever get up and run again.

"But You were there for me. Perhaps no truth in Hebrews has touched me more deeply than that of Your grace and its power to strengthen."

I reach for my Bible. It opens to Hebrews of its own accord. As I turn the pages my thoughts soar.

"Lord, the theme of this book is the superiority of Jesus Christ. You say it over and over again in so many different ways.

"The message is that Christianity is practical. You want me to take it into my home, my church, my community.

"The goal is spiritual maturity. Not just for me, but for all Your children.

"And over and around and throughout the book You've placed Your grace—the new covenant of Jesus' blood. It's a crimson thread that binds us all together. And what is grace but God doing for us what we can't do by ourselves.

My eye catches on Hebrews 13:5—"I will never leave you nor forsake you." The words of God's promise is filled with His grace.

"I will not, I will not, I will not"

Kenneth Wuest has something significant to say about this verse in his book *Word Studies in Hebrews*. He writes that the word *forsake* is a compound of three Greek words. One word means the idea of forsaking one; another suggests rejection, defeat, helplessness; the other refers to some place or circumstance in which a person may find himself helpless and forsaken.

He then said that these three negatives before the promise make it one of triple assurance. *"I will not, I will not, I will not let thee down, leave thee in the lurch, leave thee destitute, leave thee in straits and helpless, abandon thee."*[6]

I see these three *will nots* as the strengthening power of grace. Grace—behind us, ahead of us, surrounding us. It's the power that keeps us growing toward spiritual maturity. It's what enables us to run

---

6. Kenneth S. Wuest, *Word Studies in Hebrews* (Grand Rapids, MI: Wm. B. Eerdmans Publishing Company, 1947), p. 234.

Grace Be with You All . . .

and keep running until we cross into that eternal rest—the heavenly Jerusalem.

Up, Up, and Away

My thoughts return to my traveler. She's taking off again. She's soaring into the sky. But this time she's taking something with her.

She's done more than read the book of Hebrews. She's studied. She's observed. She's seen the parts that make up the whole of its message and applied its truth to her life.

That message has become a part of who she is. She's ready now to take that message to others.

Grace be with you all.
The Shepherd who became the Lamb is Lord of all.
And we are the sheep of His pasture.